GRILL RECIPES COOKBOOK FOR BEGINNERS AND EXPERTS

GUIDE TO PREPARING SIMPLE, HEALTHY, AND DELICIOUS MEALS WITH YOUR GRILL

By

Roberto DEL RIO

TABLE OF CONTENS

INTRODUCTION

According to science, grilling is a fast, dry heat cooking process that uses "a significant amount of direct radiant heat. Direct conduction heating is used when frying in a pan, while thermal radiation is used during frying. Let's talk about frying or grilling. Cooking food on the grill over a heat source, such as ceramic containers heated by gas flames or a fire produced by burning coal, is called grilling. Direct heat easily burns the outside of the food, maintaining strong and sometimes satisfyingly charred flavors, as well as looking good with an appetizing crust. When food is cooked over medium heat, it develops a smokier crust and flavor. Grilling allows you to cook vegetables and meat in a short time, and is perfect for daily and weekly use. Grilling uses a phenomenon known as thermal radiation. The heat source can be more or less than the one you are cooking, but when it is higher than the temperature of the food it is generally referred to as "grilling". Most grills are heated from below. Why grill food quickly? Because the high temperatures and heat are used near where the food is placed for cooking. The energy source that powers the "Grill" Energy reaches the food in a different way during the cooking phase without having to pass through a liquid or a quantity of air. The amount of heat absorbed by food is determined by its surface: darker foods absorb infrared rays more easily than lighter foods that reflect less heat.

THINGS TO KEEP IN MIND WHEN GRILLING

START THE GRILL CORRECTLY.

The specific indications and times for preheating are available in the Grill manual. Then carefully read the manual of the Grill in use. In general, it takes longer to heat a charcoal grill than a gas grill.

CHARCOAL GRILLS

It takes about 20 minutes to heat the charcoal grill, so the heat needs to be adjusted according to what you intend to prepare. Make sure you throw away the ashes. Open all vents on the bottom of the grill to allow for the full airflow needed to ventilate the flame. Follow the guide to turn on the grill. You can use: old newspapers, fireplaces or special liquids for grilling to be ignited with a lighter. To use the right amount of material to light the grill, always follow the specific instruction manual.

GAS GRILL

Since gas grills heat up quickly, it will only take 10 minutes to preheat the grill before cooking the food. When the grill is on, do not close the lid. Open the valve on the propane gas tank. Then, turn on one of the hob burners. After turning on the first stove, you can turn on all the burners available and the tools needed to prepare the food to be grilled.

KEEP THE GRILL CLEAN

Preheat the grill for 10-15 minutes (using direct or indirect heat) with all burners on. Any residual material from the previous firing that has been incinerated must be removed. Then clean the grill and the burners used for cooking with a special grill brush with brass bristles. Steel bristles damage the enamel finish of some grids. (If you do not have a brass-bristled cleaning brush, clean the grates with a crumpled ball of durable aluminum foil held between the tongs.) Thoroughly clean the grates to make sure they are smooth and free of food, debris, and ashes related to the recent grilling. After each grilling, it is necessary to clean before preheating. Preheat the grill for one hour with all burners on (clean before starting the preheating phase)

GREASE THE FOOD BEFORE COOKING

Brush the food with cooking oil or spray where possible to encourage caramelization and those classic grill marks, as well as to prevent the food from sticking to the grill itself. If you don't grease the food before grilling it, the natural juices can evaporate and the food will be dry. Greasing is especially recommended when grilling vegetables.

CHECK THE HEAT OF THE GRILL

On a gas powered grill, maintaining a fixed temperature is easy by adjusting the knob to the desired heat level. Vents are very important for regulating the heat on a charcoal grill. The support surfaces of the dishes during the grilling phase must not be positioned close to each other to the vents at the bottom of the grille. This is to allow for proper air flow. The vents on the top of the grille should also be slightly open. The more the vents are open, the hotter the grill will cook. The vents should be covered about half of their opening if moderate heat is desired.

BEFORE COOKING THE FOOD, CHECK THE SIZE OF ITS "CUT" WHICH MUST BE IN LINE WITH THE SPACE AVAILABLE ON THE GRILL.

If there is not enough space on the hob, it is useless to buy a large cut of meat, such as a roast or shoulder because they will not cook. So always remember that grilling always requires adequate air ventilation.

NEVER USE PLASTIC UTENSILS FOR GRILLING

Always use metal or silicone-coated utensils. The plastic may melt if exposed to the high heat of the grill and mix with the food being cooked.

WHEN SHOULD FOOD BE COVERED WITH A LID AND WHEN SHOULD IT BE LEFT FREE AND OPEN?

Although it's tempting to double-check your food, when should you leave the grill open and when should it be closed? It's simple. The lid should be kept open when the food you are cooking is thin, such as a slice of zucchini or small asparagus. It should be closed for larger, bulkier foods such as corn on the cob, chicken breasts or thick-cut pork chops. By closing the lid, you can take advantage of the warmer fire of the grill.

GIVE THE MEAT TIME TO REST AFTER COOKING.

Allow your cooked meat to rest after cooking under a sheet of foil, which allows it to retain optimal flavor and juiciness. A chop or steak will take 5 minutes, while a huge roast will take a half hour or more. As it rests, most of the internal moisture will equalize evenly throughout the meat, ensuring that all pieces are moist and of equal quality.

ON THE GRILL, LEAVE SOME SPACE BETWEEN THE COOKING AND CONSEQUENTLY COOKED CUTS OF FOOD.

If you over place food on the cooking surface it will not cook well and will tend to boil instead of grill. Putting too much meat on the grill causes some parts of them to be shielded from direct heat and by producing steam they do not allow an optimal cooking on food surfaces. All of this will result in uneven cooking. Cuts don't require much space; for best results, leave at least an inch of clearance between each cut.

START COOKING WITH THE FOODS THAT TAKE THE LONGEST TO COOK.

Meat for example should not be overcooked. To prevent thinner cuts of food from burning, you should turn them over continuously. However if the optimal temperature has been correctly set on the grill, it is not necessary to constantly check the temperature in order to avoid raising the heat too much, with the risk of burning the food. All this processing can cause moisture loss, resulting in drier food. Wait for heat and time to do their work.

ADVANTAGES OF GRILLING

Cooking on the grill has more health benefits than cooking on the stove or in the oven. Some of the health benefits of grilling are:

LESS FAT

One of the most significant health benefits of grilling is the reduction in fat. Excess fat from the inside of foods runs off before it reaches the plate. Even cooking vegetables on the grill leads to almost total fat reduction and a perfect result. To add flavor and cooking quality, season grilled vegetables with a little good quality olive oil, and for meat use a thin layer of cooking spray that can prevent some parts of the meat from sticking. Grilling is a good idea for spending time with friends and family. In summer, grilling is a common social activity that allows people to satisfy their own needs and those of eventual guests. Taking care of the grill allows you to spend time outdoors with family and friends.

NUTRIENT-RICH MEATS

Grilled vegetables aren't the only thing that becomes more nutritious when you grill. In grilled meats, thiamine and riboflavin are significantly in higher amounts. B vitamins like riboflavin and thiamine help the body turn food into energy. Grilled meat or fish, cooked well to not burned over a gas flame, is an excellent addition to a balanced diet.

MORE NUTRITIOUS VEGETABLES

Since grilling vegetables takes less time than cooking them in a conventional oven, this leads to preserving more natural nutrients. In the cooking water, boiled or stewed vegetables leave much of their flavor behind, as well as their mineral and vitamin content. Grilled vegetables, on the other hand, retain their color and texture while gaining flavor and nutrients.

LESS BUTTER FOR COOKING

Meats cooked over an open flame retain more moisture than meats prepared in other ways. This indicates that grilling foods results in a significant reduction in the use of butter as they remain more moist. By using less butter on your meat the food will be less fatty.

1 GRILLED PEACH AND BURRATA CROSTINI

Servings: 12   **Cook Time: 15 Min**   **Prep Time 10 Min**

INGREDIENTS:
- ✓ Two balls of burrata cheese.
- ✓ 4 peaches pitted and sliced.
- ✓ 3 ½ tbsps. extra virgin olive oil
- ✓ 4 ounces prosciutto thinly sliced.
- ✓ One French or sourdough baguette slice into
- ✓ ¼ pieces. One bunch of basil leaves.
- ✓ Pepper and salt to taste.
- ✓ Balsamic vinegar if you want.

DIRECTIONS:
- ➢ Warm up the grill to moderate temperature.
- ➢ Season the peach and baguette slices with pepper and salt after brushing them with oil.
- ➢ Grill baguette for 2 minutes along each side of the grill
- ➢ Remove baguette from the grill.
- ➢ Bring peach slices to the grill

- ➢ Cook for around 2 to 3 minutes on both sides
- ➢ (Till it softened but not watery)
- ➢ Set basil on every crostini
- ➢ Top with one tbsp. or two of burrata
- ➢ Cover with a thin slice of prosciutto and a slice of grilled peach on top of the burrata
- ➢ If needed, drizzle balsamic vinegar before serving.

2 EGGS BENEDICT BURGER

Servings: 3   **Cook Time: 20 Min**   **Prep Time 30 Min**

INGREDIENTS:
FOR THE BURGERS
- ✓ 1 lb. lean ground beef Worcestershire
- ✓ 3 eggs poached or fried. Salt
- ✓ Pepper

FOR THE HOLLANDAISE SAUCE
- ✓ 1 Tablespoon water
- ✓ 1 stick unsalted butter sliced into eight pieces.
- ✓ 3 large egg yolks

- ✓ 3 slices of crispy cooked bacon.
- ✓ Burger buns or English muffins

- ✓ Juice from half lemon Salt
- ✓ Pepper

DIRECTIONS:
- ➢ Heat the grill to medium-high temperature.
- ➢ In a heatproof bowl set over a pan of boiling water
- ➢ Mix egg yolks with water, constantly mix for around five minutes till the mixture thickens.
- ➢ Take the pan off the heat and add lemon juice to it.
- ➢ Melt 1-2 slices of butter at a time, stir vigorously.
- ➢ Add pepper and salt according to your taste
- ➢ Heat over a double boiler, stir frequently
- ➢ Add 1-2 teaspoon hot water if the sauce thickens unnecessarily.

- ➢ Season the ground beef with pepper, salt, and a few drops of Worcestershire sauce.
- ➢ Shape a patty out of ground beef by slicing it into three fair parts.
- ➢ Cook for 4-5 minutes on each side on the grill or grilled to your taste.
- ➢ Add an egg, crispy bacon, and a tablespoon of hollandaise sauce on top of the buns.

3 BLUEBERRY-CINNAMON BREAD

Servings: 8   Cook Time: 35 Min   Prep Time 15 Min

INGREDIENTS:

- ✓ Six large eggs
- ✓ 1 cup 2 percent milk or half-and-half cream
- ✓ Half cup chopped toasted pecans.
- ✓ 2 tbsps. maple syrup
- ✓ 1 loaf (1 pound) cinnamon-raisin bread
- ✓ 1 tsp. vanilla extract
- ✓ Two cups divided fresh blueberries.

DIRECTIONS:

- ➤ Set grill on low heat or prepare campfire
- ➤ Assemble bread slices on a double-thickness piece of heavy-duty foil greased (about 24x18 in.)
- ➤ Wrap the foil around the sides of the pan, keeping the top open
- ➤ Mix the milk, syrup, vanilla, and eggs in a bowl
- ➤ Pour over the bread and cover with 1 cup of blueberries and nuts
- ➤ Fold the top edges over and crimp to cover.
- ➤ Cook for 30-40 minutes on a grill grate over a campfire or grill
- ➤ (Until eggs are cooked through)
- ➤ Remove from the heat and set aside for 10 minutes
- ➤ Serve additional maple syrup and remaining blueberries.

4 MASALA GRILLED TOAST

Servings: 4 Sandwiches   Cook Time: 2 Min   Prep Time 5 Min

INGREDIENTS:

- ✓ 1 tablespoon butter or oil for coating bread
- ✓ 8 slices of bread.
- ✓ Half capsicum chopped.

FOR TOMATO KETCHUP MIXTURE

- ✓ 1 teaspoon oregano or Italian seasoning
- ✓ Half teaspoon Chat masala
- ✓ Salt to taste

- ✓ 4 teaspoons cheese spread you can increase or decrease as your desired taste.
- ✓ 1 onion minced

- ✓ 4 teaspoons tomato ketchup
- ✓ 1/4 teaspoon red chili powder optional

DIRECTIONS:

FOR FILLING.

- ➤ Combine all of the ingredients for the tomato ketchup mixture in a mixing bowl.
- ➤ Add the diced vegetables.
- ➤ Taste it and customize the flavors to your choice

FOR GRILLING

- ➤ Spread tomato sauce mixture on one slice of bread.
- ➤ Place cheese spread on the other slice and cover with the first slice.
- ➤ Brush bread slices with a thin covering of butter or oil before grilling.

- ➤ Cook in the griller, or on a Tawa, or in a sandwich maker.
- ➤ Tasty Delicious Crispy Masala Grilled
- ➤ Toast will be ready in around 2 minutes
- ➤ (Or when both sides have become crispy)
- ➤ Serve hot and enjoy the toasts.

5 GRILLED CINNAMON FRENCH TOAST

Servings: 5 Slices **Cook Time: 15 Min** **Prep Time 15 Min**

INGREDIENTS:

- ✓ 5 slices of day-old bread, sourdough used. Blend these for liquid:
- ✓ 1 1/2 tablespoon non-dairy milk (room temperature, not chilled)
- ✓ 1 teaspoon maple syrup (grade B)
- ✓ 1 teaspoon extra virgin coconut oil.
- ✓ Pinch of salt.
- ✓ 1 ripe banana.

- ✓ 6 ounces silken tofu
- ✓ 1/4 teaspoon fresh orange zest
- ✓ 1/4 teaspoon cinnamon
- ✓ Pinch of vanilla bean (if you want)
- ✓ Peanut butter maple spread:
- ✓ 1 tablespoon nut butter, softened plus
- ✓ 1 teaspoon maple syrup (grade B)
- ✓ Orange zest and cinnamon for seasoning on top

DIRECTIONS:

- ➤ Heat the nut butter and mix it with the maple syrup; set aside.
- ➤ In a blender, mix the liquid ingredients
- ➤ Combine them until the mixture become smooth
- ➤ Add the liquid into a shallow flat dish, such as a small casserole dish.
- ➤ If you're using conventional cooking techniques
- ➤ Heat your skillet or panini press on the stove
- ➤ Add a few amounts of coconut oil to the warm surface to grease things up.
- ➤ Soak the first slice of bread for around five seconds on both sides
- ➤ After that, bring it on a hot cooking surface
- ➤ You can cook one at a time or till the grill/skillet is loaded

- ➤ Make sure there is enough distance between the slices for them to cook
- ➤ Drizzle with some orange zest and cinnamon on the toasted side that is facing up.
- ➤ Cook for about 2-3 minutes of the first side
- ➤ Then flip it with a large spatula
- ➤ Cook for an additional 2-3 minutes
- ➤ If you're using a panini press
- ➤ Press down gently for about a minute to hold in those grill marks
- ➤ (This move is optional).
- ➤ Set on a plate and top with maple syrup and nut butter spread. Enjoy!

6 BREAKFAST SAUSAGE

Servings: 2 Slices   **Cook Time: 10 Min**   **Prep Time 30 Min**

INGREDIENTS:

FOR TEST PATTY:

- ✓ 1 tsp. Vegetable oil

FOR THE SAUSAGE:

- ✓ 2 tsps. kosher salt
- ✓ 1 1/2 tsps. Ground black pepper.
- ✓ 2 tsps. Chopped fresh sage leaves
- ✓ 2 tsps. Chopped fresh thyme leaves.
- ✓ Half pound fatback cut into 1/2-inch cubes.
- ✓ Two pounds trimmed boneless pork butt, cut into 1/2-inch cubes

- ✓ Half tsp chopped fresh rosemary leaves.
- ✓ 1 tbsp light brown sugar
- ✓ Half tsp grated nutmeg
- ✓ Half tsp Cayenne pepper
- ✓ 1/2 tsp Red pepper flakes

DIRECTIONS:

- ➢ In a medium bowl, add salt, pepper, rosemary, thyme
- ➢ Them nutmeg, cayenne, pork butt, pepper flakes, sage, and fatback and mix it well
- ➢ Put it in the refrigerator for at least one hour.
- ➢ Grind the mixture in a grinder.
- ➢ In a small skillet, heat one tsp. of oil over moderate flame
- ➢ Cook 1 tbsp. Sized patty of sausage mixture in the hot oil and cook it
- ➢ (Uuntil there appears brown color on the patty)
- ➢ Taste the patty and customize the salt and spices if required
- ➢ Make 3-ounce patties that are about 1/2-inch thick and 3-inches wide.

- ➢ Build the charcoal fire in one of the chimneys
- ➢ Pour out and scatter the coals uniformly over the coal grate's entire surface
- ➢ (Until all the charcoal is burned and covered in grey ash)
- ➢ Preheat for 5 minutes after placing the cooking grate and covering the gill
- ➢ The cooking grate must be washed and oiled
- ➢ Grill patties over high temperature
- ➢ (Until browned and cooked through, about 7 to 10 minutes total, flipping halfway through)
- ➢ Remove the patties from the grill
- ➢ Set them aside for 3 minutes to rest before serving.

7 BREAKFAST SKEWERS

Servings: 5   **Cook Time: 10 Min**   **Prep Time 10 Min**

INGREDIENTS:

- ✓ 1 package (7 ounces) frozen fully cooked breakfast sausage links, Defrosted.
- ✓ Ten medium fresh mushrooms
- ✓ 2 tbsps. melted butter.
- ✓ 1 can (20 ounces) drained pineapple chunks
- ✓ Maple syrup

DIRECTIONS:

- ➢ Slice the sausages in half
- ➢ On the other hand, thread sausages, pineapple, mushrooms on five soaked wooden or metal skewers
- ➢ Brush with maple syrup and butter.
- ➢ Grill, uncover, over moderate flame for 8 minutes
- ➢ Flip, and basting with syrup, for eight minutes
- ➢ (Or till the sausages are golden brown and fruit is cooked through)

8 GRILLED FRIED EGGS

Servings: 3 **Cook Time: 5 Min** **Prep Time 2 Min**

INGREDIENTS:
- ✓ Aluminum foil
- ✓ 3 Eggs
- ✓ Black Pepper and salt
- ✓ Vegetable oil or cooking spray.

DIRECTIONS:
- ➢ Preheat the grill to moderate temperature (180C/350F).
- ➢ Make a small round tray or boat out of aluminum foil for each egg
- ➢ Fold a foil piece (approximately 13 x 30 cm/5 x 12 inches) in half to do this
- ➢ Curve up the edge of the double-thick foil to form a rim
- ➢ Then fold over as required to create a round tray about 4 inches (10 cm) in diameter.
- ➢ Brush the trays' bottoms with oil or spray them with cooking spray

NOTES:
- ➢ To make it easier, crack each egg first into a small cup
- ➢ Then add to the tray.
- ➢ If you want to cook an over-easy egg
- ➢ Use a significantly wider tray so you can conveniently slide a flipper under the egg as the white starts to set

- ➢ Preheat the grill and put the trays on it. In every tray, crack an egg.
- ➢ Cover and cook for a few minutes, or till the egg white part begin to set
- ➢ If you want a soft yolk, remove the lid and cook for another 2 to 3 minutes
- ➢ (Or till the eggs are ready to your taste)
- ➢ Close the lid if you want solid yolk.
- ➢ Take off the eggs from the grill and season with salt and pepper.

- ➢ Cook for around a minute on the other side.
- ➢ Create wider oval-shaped foil trays for a two-egg filling.
- ➢ Use a wide sheet of foil with the side curved up to grill more eggs at once
- ➢ Brush the foil with oil or cooking spray before putting it

9 SMOKED AND PULLED BEEF

Servings: 6   **Cook Time: 6 H**   **Prep Time 10 Min**

INGREDIENTS:

- ✓ 4 lb. beef sirloin tip roast
- ✓ 1/2 cup BBQ rub

- ✓ bottles of amber beer
- ✓ 1 bottle barbecues sauce

DIRECTIONS:

- ➢ Turn your wood pellet grill on smoke
- ➢ Set then trim excess fat from the steak.
- ➢ Coat the steak with grill rub
- ➢ Let it smoke on the grill for 1 hour.
- ➢ Continue cooking and flipping the steak for the next 3 hours
- ➢ Transfer the steak to a braising vessel. Add the beers.

- ➢ Braise the beef until tender
- ➢ Then transfer to a platter reserving 2 cups of cooking liquid.
- ➢ Use a pair of forks to shred the beef and return it to the pan
- ➢ Add the reserved liquid and barbecue sauce
- ➢ Stir well and keep warm before serving.Enjoy.

10 REVERSE SEARED FLANK STEAK

Servings: 2   **Cook Time: 10 Min**   **Prep Time 10 Min**

INGREDIENTS:

- ✓ 1.5 lb. Flanks steak
- ✓ 1 tbsp. salt
- ✓ 1/2 onion powder

- ✓ 1/4 tbsp. garlic powder
- ✓ 1/2 black pepper, coarsely ground

DIRECTIONS:

- ➢ Preheat your wood pellet grill to 225f
- ➢ In a mixing bowl, mix salt, onion powder, garlic powder
- ➢ Add, and pepper. Generously rub the steak with the mixture.
- ➢ Place the steaks on the preheated grill
- ➢ Close the lid and let the steak cook.
- ➢ Crank up the grill to high then let it heat

- ➢ The steak should be off the grill
- ➢ Tend with foil to keep it warm.
- ➢ Once the grill is heated up to 450°F, place the steak back
- ➢ Grill for 3 minutes per side.
- ➢ Remove from heat, pat with butter, and serve. Enjoy.

11 GRILLED BUTTER BASTED PORTERHOUSE STEAK

Servings 4   **Cook Time: 40 Min**   **Prep Time 10 Min**

INGREDIENTS:

- ✓ 4 tbsp. butter, melted
- ✓ 2 tbsp. Worcestershire sauce
- ✓ 2 tbsp. Dijon mustard
- ✓ Griller Prime rib rub

DIRECTIONS:

- ➢ Set your wood pellet grill to 225°F with the lid closed for 15 minutes.
- ➢ In a mixing bowl, mix butter, sauce, Dijon mustard until smooth
- ➢ Brush the mixture on the meat then season with the rub.
- ➢ Arrange the meat on the grill grate and cook for 30 minutes

- ➢ Transfer the meat to a pattern then increase the heat to high.
- ➢ Return the meat to the grill grate to grill
- ➢ (Until your desired doneness is achieved)
- ➢ Baste with the butter mixture again if you desire
- ➢ Let rest for 3 minutes before serving. Enjoy.

12 COCOA CRUSTED GRILLED FLANK STEAK

Servings: 6   **Cook Time: 6 Min**   **Prep Time 10 Min**

INGREDIENTS:

- ✓ 1 tbsp. cocoa powder
- ✓ 2 tbsp. chili powder
- ✓ 1 tbsp. chipotle chili powder
- ✓ 1/2 tbsp. garlic powder
- ✓ 1/2 tbsp. onion powder
- ✓ 1-1/2 tbsp. brown sugar
- ✓ 1 tbsp. cumin
- ✓ 1 tbsp. smoked paprika
- ✓ 1 tbsp. kosher salt
- ✓ 1/2 tbsp. black pepper
- ✓ Olive oil
- ✓ 4 lb. Flank steak

DIRECTIONS:

- ➢ Whisk together cocoa, chili powder, garlic powder
- ➢ Add, onion powder, sugar, cumin, paprika, salt, and pepper in a mixing bowl.
- ➢ Drizzle the steak with oil then rub with the cocoa mixture on both sides.
- ➢ Preheat your wood pellet grill for 15 minutes with the lid closed.
- ➢ Cook the meat on the grill grate for 5 minutes
- ➢ (Or until the internal temperature reaches 135°F)
- ➢ Remove the meat from the grill
- ➢ Let it cool for 15 minutes to allow the juices to redistribute.
- ➢ Slice the meat against the grain and on a sharp diagonal.
- ➢ Serve and enjoy.

13 SUPPER BEEF ROAST

Servings: 7   **Cook Time: 3 H**   **Prep Time 5 Min**

INGREDIENTS:

- ✓ 3-1/2 beef top round
- ✓ 3 tbsp. vegetable oil
- ✓ Prime rib rub
- ✓ 2 cups beef broth
- ✓ One russet potato peeled and sliced
- ✓ Two carrots peeled and sliced.
- ✓ Two celery stalks, chopped
- ✓ One onion, sliced.
- ✓ Two thyme sprigs

DIRECTIONS:

- ➢ Rub the roast with vegetable oil
- ➢ Place it on the roasting fat side up
- ➢ Season with prime rib rub, then pours the beef broth.
- ➢ Set the temperature to 500°F
- ➢ Preheat the wood pellet grill for 15 minutes with the lid closed.
- ➢ Cook for 30 minutes or until the roast is well seared.
- ➢ Reduce temperature to 225°F
- ➢ Add the veggies and thyme and cover with foil
- ➢ Cook for three more hours
- ➢ (Or until the internal temperature reaches 135°F)
- ➢ Remove from the grill and let rest for 10 minutes
- ➢ Slice against the grain
- ➢ Serve with vegetables and the pan drippings.Enjoy.

14 BACON-SWISS CHEESESTEAK MEATLOAF

Servings: 10   **Cook Time: 2 H**   **Prep Time 15 Min**

INGREDIENTS:

- ✓ 1 tablespoon canola oil
- ✓ 2 garlic cloves finely chopped.
- ✓ 1 medium onion finely chopped.
- ✓ 1 poblano chile, stemmed, seeded, and finely chopped.
- ✓ 2 pounds extra-lean ground beef
- ✓ 2 tablespoons Montreal steak seasoning
- ✓ 1 tablespoon A.1. Steak Sauce
- ✓ ½ pound bacon, cooked and crumbled.
- ✓ 2 cups shredded Swiss cheese.
- ✓ 1 egg, beaten.
- ✓ 2 cups breadcrumbs
- ✓ ½ cup Tiger Sauce

DIRECTIONS:

- ➢ On your stove top, heat the canola oil in a medium sauté pan over medium-high heat
- ➢ Add the garlic, onion, and poblano, and sauté for 3 to 5 minutes
- ➢ (Or until the onion is just barely translucent)
- ➢ Supply your smoker with wood pellets and follow the manufacturer's specific start-up procedure
- ➢ Preheat, with the lid closed to 225°F.
- ➢ In a large bowl, combine the sautéed vegetables, ground beef
- ➢ Then steak seasoning, steak sauce, bacon, Swiss cheese, egg, and breadcrumbs
- ➢ Mix with your hands until well incorporated, then shape into a loaf.
- ➢ Put the meatloaf in a cast iron skillet and place it on the grill
- ➢ Insert meat thermometer inserted in the loaf reads 165°F.
- ➢ Top with the meatloaf with the Tiger Sauce
- ➢ Remove from the gril
- ➢ Let rest for about 10 minutes before serving.

15 GRILLED PORK TENDERLOIN, TRAWBERRIES AND ROSEMARY

Servings: 4   **Cook Time: 50 Min**   **Prep Time 10 Min**

INGREDIENTS:

- ✓ One and a half tsp. salt One teaspoon pepper
- ✓ One to two tsp. fresh rosemary Three garlic cloves
- ✓ One tbsp. olive oil
- ✓ One pound pork tenderloin Quarter cup balsamic vinegar Quarter cup olive oil
- ✓ One small shallot that is finely chopped (two tablespoons) A pinch of salt & pepper
- ✓ One tsp. squeeze of lemon juice

GARNISH:

- ✓ One cup of diced strawberries, glaze or balsamic reduction and rosemary sprigs (fresh)
- ✓ Two cups strawberries- small diced
- ✓ Half cup white wine
- ✓ Two tbsp. sugar

DIRECTIONS:

- ➢ In a blender, mix the marinade ingredients together
- ➢ In a big Ziplock bag
- ➢ (You may also use a shallow baking dish)
- ➢ Put the loin and marinade, covering all the sides
- ➢ Refrigerate overnight or for 1 hour.
- ➢ Heat the oil on a medium-low temperature in a small pot
- ➢ Then add the shallot. Stir & sauté for around 2 to 3 minutes, until golden
- ➢ Garnish with wine, sugar, strawberries, salt, and pepper
- ➢ Just bring it to a simmer
- ➢ On medium-low heat, continue to simmer until the wine has decreased and the strawberries have become thickened for around 10 minutes
- ➢ It's supposed to look like some loose jam
- ➢ Add lemon squeeze. And put aside.
- ➢ Preheat the grill to a high temperature.
- ➢ Take the loin from the marinade & pour in a little pot some extra marinade
- ➢ You will use this cooked marinade for basting the loin
- ➢ Boil for 1 minute or till it is darkened.
- ➢ Scrape it clean once the grill gets hot
- ➢ Turn it to med-high & put the pork loin straight on the grill
- ➢ Cook every 3 minutes for a total of 12 minutes, rotating and basting
- ➢ In-between the turns, cover
- ➢ Control temperature during the process as per your requirement
- ➢ Continue to cook on the grill and, if necessary
- ➢ Reduce heat or complete it in the oven until the loin reaches around 140-degree F at the thickest point
- ➢ Allow 5 to 10 minutes to rest.
- ➢ Slice loin into 3/4 inch slices once ready to eat
- ➢ Then plate it, topping it with compotes (or place the pork over compote)
- ➢ Use rosemary sprigs, fresh diced strawberries & balsamic reduction for garnishing.

16 EXPLOSIVE SMOKY BACON

Servings: 10   **Cook Time: 2h 10 Min**   **Prep Time 20 Min**

INGREDIENTS:

- ✓ 1-pound thick cut bacon
- ✓ One tablespoon Grill spice rub
- ✓ 2 pounds bulk pork sausage
- ✓ 1 cup cheddar cheese, shredded.
- ✓ Four garlic cloves, minced.
- ✓ 18 ounces Grill sauce

DIRECTIONS:

- ➤ Take your drip pan and add water, cover with aluminum foil.
- ➤ Pre-heat your smoker to 225 degrees F
- ➤ Use water fill water pan halfway through and place it over drip pan.
- ➤ Add wood chips to the side tray.
- ➤ Reserve about ½ a pound of your bacon for cooking later
- ➤ Lay 2 strips of your remaining bacon on a clean surface in an X formation.
- ➤ Alternate the horizontal and vertical bacon strips by waving them tightly in an over and under to create a lattice-like pattern.
- ➤ Sprinkle one teaspoon of Grill rub over the woven bacon
- ➤ Arrange ½ a pound of your bacon in a large-sized skillet
- ➤ Cook them for 10 minutes over medium-high heat.
- ➤ Drain the cooked slices on a kitchen towel and crumble them.
- ➤ Place your sausages in a large-sized re-sealable bag.
- ➤ While the sausages are still in the bag, roll them out to a square that has the same sized as the woven bacon.
- ➤ Cut off the bag from the sausage and arrange them sausage over the woven bacon.
- ➤ Toss away the bag.
- ➤ Sprinkle some crumbled bacon, green onions, cheddar cheese, and garlic over the rolled sausages.
- ➤ Pour about ¾ bottle of your Grill sauce over the sausage and season with some more BBQ rub.
- ➤ Roll up the woven bacon tightly all around the sausage, forming a loaf.
- ➤ Cook the bacon-sausage loaf in your smoker for about one and a ½ hour.
- ➤ Brush up the woven bacon with remaining
- ➤ Grill sauce and keep smoking for about 30 minutes
- ➤ (Until the center of the loaf is no longer pink)
- ➤ Use an instant thermometer to check if the internal temperature is at least 165 degrees Fahrenheit.
- ➤ If yes, then take it out and let it rest for 30 minutes.
- ➤ Slice and serve!

17 MAPLE-SMOKED PORK CHOPS

Servings: 4   **Cook Time: 55 Min**   **Prep Time 15 Min**

INGREDIENTS:

- ✓ 4 (8-ounce) pork chops, bone-in or boneless (I use boneless)
- ✓ Salt
- ✓ Freshly ground black pepper

DIRECTIONS:

- ➤ Supply your smoker with wood pellets and follow the manufacturer's specific start-up procedure.
- ➤ Drizzle pork chop with salt and pepper to season.
- ➤ Place the chops directly on the grill grate and smoke for 30 minutes.
- ➤ Increase the grill's temperature to 350°F
- ➤ Continue to cook the chops until their internal temperature reaches 145°F.
- ➤ Remove the pork chops from the grill
- ➤ Let them rest for 5 minutes before serving.

18 APPLE-SMOKED PORK TENDERLOIN

Servings: 6   Cook Time: 5 H   Prep Time 15 Min

INGREDIENTS:
- ✓ 2 (1-pound) pork tenderloins
- ✓ 1 batch Not-Just-for-Pork Rub

DIRECTIONS:
- ➤ Supply your smoker with wood pellets
- ➤ Follow the manufacturer's specific start-up procedure
- ➤ Preheat the grill.
- ➤ Generously season the tenderloins with the rub. W
- ➤ Put tenderloins on the grill and smoke for 4 or 5 hours
- ➤ (Until their internal temperature reaches 145°F)
- ➤ The tenderloins must be put out of the grill
- ➤ Let it rest for 5-10 minutes
- ➤ Then begin slicing into thin pieces before serving.

19 LOVABLE PORK BELLY

Servings: 4   Cook Time: 4 H 30 Min   Prep Time 15 Min

INGREDIENTS:
- ✓ 5 pounds of pork belly
- ✓ 1 cup dry rub

FOR SAUCE
- ✓ Two tablespoons honey
- ✓ Three tablespoons butter

- ✓ Three tablespoons olive oil

- ✓ 1 cup Grill sauce

DIRECTIONS:
- ➤ Take your drip pan and add water
- ➤ Cover with aluminum foil.
- ➤ Pre-heat your smoker to 250 degrees F
- ➤ Add pork cubes, dry rub, olive oil into a bowl and mix well.
- ➤ Use water fill water pan halfway through and place it over drip pan.
- ➤ Add wood chips to the side tray.
- ➤ Transfer pork cubes to your smoker and smoke for 3 hours (covered)

- ➤ Remove pork cubes from the smoker and transfer to foil pan
- ➤ Add honey, butter, Grill sauce, and stir.
- ➤ Cover the pan with foil and move back to a smoker
- ➤ Smoke for 90 minutes more.
- ➤ Remove foil and smoke for 15 minutes more until the sauce thickens.
- ➤ Serve and enjoy!

20 WOW-PORK TENDERLOIN

Servings: 4   Cook Time: 3 H   Prep Time 15 Min

INGREDIENTS:
- ✓ One pork tenderloin
- ✓ ¼ cup Grill sauce

- ✓ Three tablespoons dry rub

DIRECTIONS:
- ➤ Take your drip pan and add water.
- ➤ Cover with aluminum foil.
- ➤ Pre-heat your smoker to 225 degrees F
- ➤ Rub the spice blend all finished the pork tenderloin.
- ➤ Use water fill water pan halfway through
- ➤ Place it over drip pan.
- ➤ Add wood chips to the side tray.

- ➤ Transfer pork meat to your smoker and smoke for 3 hours
- ➤ (Until the internal temperature reaches 145 degrees F)
- ➤ Brush the Grill sauce over pork and let it rest.
- ➤ Serve and enjoy!

21 AWESOME PORK SHOULDER

Servings: 4 **Cook Time: 12 H** **Prep Time 15 Min + 24 H**

INGREDIENTS:

- ✓ 8 pounds of pork shoulder

FOR RUB

- ✓ One teaspoon dry mustard
- ✓ One teaspoon black pepper
- ✓ One teaspoon cumin
- ✓ One teaspoon oregano
- ✓ One teaspoon cayenne pepper

- ✓ 1/3 cup salt
- ✓ ¼ cup garlic powder
- ✓ ½ cup paprika
- ✓ 1/3 cup brown sugar
- ✓ 2/3 cup sugar

DIRECTIONS:

- ➤ Bring your pork under salted water for 18 hours.
- ➤ Pull the pork out from the brine and let it sit for 1 hour.
- ➤ Rub mustard all over the pork.
- ➤ Take a bowl and mix all rub ingredients.
- ➤ Rub mixture all over the meat.
- ➤ Wrap meat and leave it overnight.
- ➤ Take your drip pan and add water. Cover with aluminum foil

- ➤ Pre-heat your smoker to 250 degrees F
- ➤ Use water fill water pan halfway through and place it over drip pan
- ➤ Add wood chips to the side tray.
- ➤ Transfer meat to smoker and smoke for 6 hours
- ➤ Take the pork out and wrap in foil, smoke for 6 hours more at 195 degrees F.
- ➤ Shred and serve. Enjoy!

22 ALABAMA PULLED PIG PORK

Servings: 8 **Cook Time: 12 H** **Prep Time 1 H**

INGREDIENTS:

- ✓ 2 cups of soy sauce
- ✓ 1 cup of Worcestershire sauce 1 cup of cranberry grape juice
- ✓ 1 cup of teriyaki sauce
- ✓ One tablespoon of hot pepper sauce

- ✓ Two tablespoons of steak sauce
- ✓ 1 cup of light brown sugar
- ✓ ½ a teaspoon of ground black pepper
- ✓ 2 pound of flank steak cut up into ¼ inch slices.

DIRECTIONS:

- ➤ Take a non-reactive saucepan
- ➤ Add cider, salt, vinegar, brown sugar, cayenne pepper, black pepper, and butter.
- ➤ Bring the mix to a boil over medium-high heat.
- ➤ Add in water and return the mixture to a boil.
- ➤ Carefully rub the pork with the sauce
- ➤ Take your drip pan and add water. Cover with aluminum foil.
- ➤ Pre-heat your smoker to 225 degrees F
- ➤ Use water fill water pan halfway through and place it over drip pan.
- ➤ Add wood chips to the side tray.
- ➤ Smoke meat for about 6-10 hours
- ➤ Make sure to keep basting it with the sauce every hour or so.

- ➤ After the first smoking is done, take an aluminum foil
- ➤ Wrap up the meat forming a watertight seal.
- ➤ Place the meat in the middle of your foil
- ➤ Bring the edges to the top, cupping up the meat complete.
- ➤ Pour 1 cup of sauce over the beef and tight it up.
- ➤ Place the package back into your smoker and smoke for 2 hours
- ➤ (Until the meat quickly pulls off from the bone)
- ➤ Once done, remove it from the smoker and pull off the pork, discarding the bone and fat
- ➤ Place the meat chunks in a pan
- ➤ Pour 1 cup of sauce for every4 pound of meat.
- ➤ Heat until simmering and serve immediately!

23 *GRILLED PORK BURGERS*

Servings: 6   **Cook Time: 1 H**   **Prep Time 15 Min**

INGREDIENTS:
- ✓ 1 beaten egg
- ✓ ¾ cup of soft breadcrumbs
- ✓ ¾ cup of grated parmesan cheese
- ✓ 1 tbsp. of dried parsley
- ✓ 2 tsp. of dried basil
- ✓ ½ tsp. of salt to taste
- ✓ ½ tsp. of garlic powder
- ✓ ¼ tsp. of pepper to taste
- ✓ 2 pounds of ground pork 6 hamburger buns

TOPPINGS:
- ✓ Lettuce leaves
- ✓ Sliced tomato
- ✓ Sliced sweet onion

DIRECTIONS:
- ➢ Use a large mixing bowl
- ➢ Add in the egg, breadcrumbs, cheese, parsley, basil, garlic powder, salt, and pepper to taste
- ➢ Then mix properly to combine
- ➢ Add in the ground pork, then mix properly
- ➢ Combine using clean hands
- ➢ Form about six patties out of the mixture, then set aside.
- ➢ Next, set a Wood Pellet smoker and grill to smoke (250 degrees F)
- ➢ Then let it fire up for about five minutes
- ➢ Place the patties on the grill and smoke for about thirty minutes
- ➢ Flip the patties over, increase the grill's temperature to 300 degrees F
- ➢ Then grill the cakes for a few minutes until an inserted thermometer reads 160 degrees F.
- ➢ Serve the pork burgers on the buns, lettuce, tomato, and onion.

24 *GRILL PORK CROWN ROAST*

Servings: 5   **Cook Time: 60 Min**   **Prep Time 5 Min**

INGREDIENTS:
- ✓ 13 ribs pork
- ✓ 1/4 cup favorite rub
- ✓ 1 cup apple juice
- ✓ 1 cup Apricot Grill sauce

DIRECTIONS:
- ➢ Set the temperature to 375°F to preheat for 15 minutes with the lid closed.
- ➢ Meanwhile, season the pork with the rub, then let sit for 30 minutes.
- ➢ Wrap the tips of each crown roast with foil to prevent the burns from turning black.
- ➢ Place the meat on the grill grate
- ➢ Cook for 90 minutes. Spray apple juice every 30 minutes.
- ➢ Remove the foils when the meat has reached an interior temperature of 125 ° F.
- ➢ Spray the roast with apple juice again
- ➢ Let cook until the internal temperature has reached 135°F.
- ➢ In the last 10 minutes of cooking, baste the roast with Grill sauce.
- ➢ Remove from the grill and wrap with foil
- ➢ Let rest for 15 minutes before serving. Enjoy.

25 COCOA CRUSTED PORK TENDERLOIN

Servings: 5 **Cook Time: 25 Min** **Prep Time 30 Min**

INGREDIENTS:
- ✓ One pork tenderloin
- ✓ 1/2 tbsp. fennel, ground
- ✓ 1 tbsp. cocoa powder, unsweetened
- ✓ 1 tbsp. smoked paprika
- ✓ 1/2 tbsp. kosher salt
- ✓ 1/2 tbsp. black pepper
- ✓ 1 tbsp. extra virgin olive oil
- ✓ Three green onion

DIRECTIONS:
- ➢ Remove the silver skin and the connective tissues from the pork loin.
- ➢ Combine the rest of the ingredients in a mixing bowl
- ➢ Then rub the mixture on the pork. Refrigerate for 30 minutes.
- ➢ Preheat the grill for 15 minutes with the lid closed.
- ➢ Sear all sides of the loin at the front of the grill
- ➢ At that point reduce the temperature to 350°F and move the pork to the center grill.
- ➢ Cook for an additional 15 minutes or until 145°F is the internal temperature.
- ➢ Remove from grill and let rest for 10 minutes before slicing. Enjoy

26 GRILLED BACON

Servings: 6 **Cook Time: 25 Min** **Prep Time 30 Min**

INGREDIENTS:
- ✓ 1 lb. bacon, thickly cut

DIRECTIONS:
- ➢ Preheat your grill to 375°F.
- ➢ Line a baking sheet with parchment paper
- ➢ Then place the bacon on it in a single layer.
- ➢ Close the lid and bake for 20 minutes
- ➢ Flip over, close the top, and bake for an additional 5 minutes.
- ➢ Serve with the favorite side and enjoy it.

27 GRILLED PORK CHOPS

Servings: 6 **Cook Time: 10 Min** **Prep Time 20 Min**

INGREDIENTS:
- ✓ Six pork chops, thickly cut
- ✓ Grill rub

DIRECTIONS:
- ➢ Preheat the grilling machine set to 450°F.
- ➢ Season the pork chops generously with the Grill rub
- ➢ Place the pork chops on the grill
- ➢ Cook for 6 minutes or until the internal temperature reaches 145°F.
- ➢ Remove from the grill and let sit for 10 minutes before serving.
- ➢ Enjoy.

28 WOOD PELLET BLACKENED PORK CHOPS

Servings: 6   **Cook Time: 20 Min**   **Prep Time 5 Min**

INGREDIENTS:
- ✓ Six pork chops
- ✓ 1/4 cup blackening seasoning
- ✓ Salt and pepper to taste

DIRECTIONS:
- ➢ Preheat your grill to 375°F.
- ➢ Meanwhile, generously season the pork chops with the blackening seasoning, salt, and pepper.
- ➢ Place the pork chops on the grill and close the lid.
- ➢ Let grill for 8 minutes, then flip the chops
- ➢ Cook until the internal temperature reaches 142°F.
- ➢ Remove the chops from the grill
- ➢ Let rest for 10 minutes before slicing.
- ➢ Serve and enjoy.

29 TERIYAKI PINEAPPLE PORK TENDERLOIN SLIDERS

Servings: 6   **Cook Time: 20 Min**   **Prep Time 20 Min**

INGREDIENTS:
- ✓ 1-1/2 lb. pork tenderloin
- ✓ One can pineapple ring
- ✓ One package king's Hawaiian rolls
- ✓ 8 oz. teriyaki sauce
- ✓ 1-1/2 tbsp. salt
- ✓ 1 tbsp. onion powder
- ✓ 1 tbsp. paprika
- ✓ 1/2 tbsp. garlic powder
- ✓ 1/2 tbsp. cayenne pepper

DIRECTIONS:
- ➢ Add all the fixings for the rub in a mixing bowl
- ➢ Mix until well mixed
- ➢ Generously rub the pork loin with the mixture.
- ➢ Heat the pellet to 325°F
- ➢ Place the meat on a grill
- ➢ Cook while you turn it every 4 minutes.
- ➢ Cook until the internal temperature reaches 145°F.
- ➢ Remove from the grill and let it rest for 5 minutes.
- ➢ Meanwhile, open the pineapple can
- ➢ Place the pineapple rings on the grill
- ➢ Flip the crews when they have a dark brown color.
- ➢ At the same time, half the rolls
- ➢ Put them on the grill and grill them until toasty browned.
- ➢ Assemble the slider by putting the bottom roll first, followed by the pork tenderloin, pineapple ring, a drizzle of sauce
- ➢ Top with the other roll half. Serve and enjoy.

30 SMOKED LAMB MEATBALLS

Servings: 20 **Cook Time: 1 H** **Prep Time 30 Min**

INGREDIENTS:

- ✓ 1 lb. lamb shoulder, ground
- ✓ 3 cloves of garlic, finely diced
- ✓ 3 tablespoon shallots, diced
- ✓ 1 tablespoon salt
- ✓ 1 egg
- ✓ ½ tablespoon pepper
- ✓ ½ tablespoon cumin
- ✓ ½ tablespoon smoked paprika
- ✓ ¼ tablespoon red pepper flakes
- ✓ ¼ tablespoon cinnamon
- ✓ ¼ cup panko breadcrumbs

DIRECTIONS:

- ➢ Set your pallet grill to 250°F.
- ➢ Combine all the ingredients in a small bowl
- ➢ Then mix thoroughly using your hands.
- ➢ Form golf ball-sized meatballs and place them on a baking sheet.
- ➢ Place the baking sheet in the smoker
- ➢ Smoke until the internal temperature reaches 160°F.
- ➢ Remove the meatballs from the smoker and serve when hot.

31 SMOKED PULLED LAMB SLIDERS

Servings: 7 **Cook Time: 9 H** **Prep Time 30 Min**

INGREDIENTS:

- ✓ 5 lb. lamb shoulder, boneless
- ✓ ½ cup olive oil
- ✓ ^{1}/3 cup kosher salt
- ✓ ^{1}/3 cup pepper, coarsely ground
- ✓ ^{1}/3 cup granulated garlic

FOR THE SPRITZ:

- ✓ 4 oz. Worcestershire sauce
- ✓ 6 oz. apple cider vinegar

DIRECTIONS:

- ➢ Preheat the oven to 225°F with a pan of water for moisture.
- ➢ Trim any excess fat from the lamb
- ➢ Then pat it dry with some paper towel
- ➢ Rub with oil, salt, pepper and garlic.
- ➢ Place the lamb in the smoker for 90 minutes
- ➢ At this point spritz every 30 minutes until the internal temperature reaches 165°F.
- ➢ Transfer the lamb to a foil pan, and then add the remaining spritz liquid
- ➢ Cover with a foil and place back in the smoker.
- ➢ Smoke until the internal temperature reaches 205°F.
- ➢ Remove from the smoker
- ➢ Let rest in a cooler without ice for 30minutes, before pulling it.
- ➢ Serve with slaw or bun and enjoy.

32 GRILLED AUSSIE LEG OF LAMB

Servings: 8   **Cook Time: 2 H**   **Prep Time 30 Min**

INGREDIENTS:

- ✓ 5 lb. Aussie Boneless Leg of lamb
- ✓ Smoked Paprika Rub:
- ✓ 1 tablespoon raw sugar
- ✓ 1 tablespoon salt
- ✓ 1 tablespoon black pepper
- ✓ 1 tablespoon smoked paprika

ROASTED CARROTS:

- ✓ 1 bunch rainbow carrots
- ✓ Olive oil

- ✓ 1 tablespoon garlic powder
- ✓ 1 tablespoon rosemary
- ✓ 1 tablespoon onion powder
- ✓ 1 tablespoon cumin
- ✓ ½ tablespoon cayenne pepper

- ✓ Salt and pepper

DIRECTIONS:

- ➢ Preheat your to 350°F and trim any excess fat from the meat.
- ➢ Combine the paprika rub ingredients and generously rub all over the meat.
- ➢ Place the lamb on the preheated smoker over indirect heat and smoke for 2 hours.
- ➢ Meanwhile, toss the carrots in oil, salt and pepper.
- ➢ Add the carrots to the grill after 1 ½ hour

- ➢ (Or until the internal temperature has reached 900°F)
- ➢ Cook until the meat's internal temperature reaches 135°F.
- ➢ Remove the lamb from the smoker
- ➢ Cover it with foil for 30 minutes.
- ➢ Once the carrots are cooked, serve with the meat and enjoy.

33 AROMATIC HERBED RACK OF LAMB

Servings: 3   **Cook Time: 2 H**   **Prep Time 30 Min**

INGREDIENTS:

- ✓ 1 tablespoons fresh sage
- ✓ 2 tablespoon fresh rosemary
- ✓ 2 tablespoon fresh thyme
- ✓ Salt and black pepper, freshly roasted, to taste
- ✓ 2 cloves of garlic, peeled
- ✓ 1 tablespoon honey
- ✓ ¼ C. olive oil
- ✓ 1 (1½-lb.) rack of lamb, trimmed

DIRECTIONS:

- ➢ In a food processor, add all ingredients except for oil and rack of lamb rack and pulse until well combined.
- ➢ While the motor is running, slowly
- ➢ Add oil and pulse until a smooth paste is formed.
- ➢ Coat the rib rack with paste generously
- ➢ Refrigerate for about 2 hours.
- ➢ Set the temperature of the Grill to 225°F and preheat with closed lid for 15 minutes.

- ➢ Arrange the rack of lamb onto the grill and cook for about 2 hours.
- ➢ Remove the rack of lamb from the grill
- ➢ Place onto a cutting board for about 10-15 minutes before slicing.
- ➢ With a sharp knife, cut the rack into individual ribs and serve.

34 SMOKED LAMB SHOULDER

Servings: 7   **Cook Time: 3 H**   **Prep Time 30 Min**

INGREDIENTS:
- ✓ 5 lb. lamb shoulder
- ✓ 1 cup cider vinegar
- ✓ 2 tablespoons oil

FOR THE SPRITZ:
- ✓ 1 cup apple cider vinegar

- ✓ 2 tablespoons kosher salt
- ✓ 2 tablespoons black pepper, freshly ground
- ✓ 1 tablespoon dried rosemary

- ✓ 1 cup apple juice

DIRECTIONS:
- ➢ Preheat the two 225°F with a pan of water for moisture.
- ➢ Trim some of the lamb's excess fat
- ➢ Rinse the meat in cold water. Pat with a paper towel to rinse.
- ➢ Inject the cider vinegar in the meat
- ➢ Then pat dry with a clean paper towel.

- ➢ Rub the meat with oil, salt, black pepper and dried rosemary
- ➢ Tie the lamb shoulder with a twine.
- ➢ Place in the smoker for an hour
- ➢ At this point spritz after every 15 minutes until the internal temperature reaches 165F.
- ➢ Remove from the smoker
- ➢ Let rest for 1 hour before shredding and serving.

35 BONELESS LEG OF LAMB

Servings: 4   **Cook Time: 4 H**   **Prep Time 30 Min**

INGREDIENTS:
- ✓ 2 ½ pounds leg of lamb, boneless, fat trimmed
- ✓ For the Marinade:
- ✓ 2 teaspoons minced garlic
- ✓ 1 tablespoon ground black pepper
- ✓ 2 tablespoons salt
- ✓ 1 teaspoon thyme
- ✓ 2 tablespoons oregano
- ✓ 2 tablespoons olive oil

DIRECTIONS:
- ➢ Take a small bowl, place all the ingredients for the marinade in it
- ➢ Then stir until combined.
- ➢ Rub the marinade on all sides of the lamb
- ➢ Then place it in a large sheet
- ➢ Cover with a plastic wrap and marinate for a minimum of 1 hour in the refrigerator.
- ➢ When ready to cook, switch on the grill
- ➢ Fill the grill hopper with apple-flavored wood pellets
- ➢ Power the grill on by using the control panel

- ➢ Select 'smoke' on the temperature dial, or set the temperature to 250°F
- ➢ Let it pre-heat for a minimum of 5 minutes.
- ➢ Meanwhile, when the grill has pre-heated, open the lid
- ➢ Put the lamb on the grill grate, shut the grill and smoke for 4 hours
- ➢ (Until the internal temperature reaches 145 degrees F)
- ➢ When done, transfer lamb to a cutting board
- ➢ Let it stand for 10 minutes, then carve it into slices and serve.

36 ELEGANT LAMB CHOPS

Servings: 4   **Cook Time: 30 Min**   **Prep Time 15 Min**

INGREDIENTS:

- ✓ 4 lamb shoulder chops
- ✓ 4 C. buttermilk
- ✓ 1 C. cold water
- ✓ ¼ C. kosher salt
- ✓ 2 tablespoons olive oil
- ✓ 1 tablespoon Texas-style rub

DIRECTIONS:

- ➢ In a large bowl, add buttermilk, water and salt, and stir until salt is dissolved.
- ➢ Add chops and coat with the mixture evenly.
- ➢ Refrigerate for at least 4 hours.
- ➢ Remove the chops from the bowl and rinse under cold running water.
- ➢ Coat the chops with olive oil and then sprinkle with rub evenly.
- ➢ Set the temperature of the Grill to 240°F
- ➢ Preheat with a closed lid for 15 minutes, using charcoal.
- ➢ Arrange the chops onto the grill and cook for about 25-30 minutes or until desired doneness.
- ➢ Meanwhile, preheat the broiler of the oven
- ➢ Grease a broiler pan.
- ➢ Remove the chops from the grill and place them onto the prepared broiler pan.
- ➢ Transfer the broiler pan into the oven
- ➢ Broil for about 3-5 minutes or until browned.
- ➢ Remove the chops from the oven and serve hot.

37 SPICY & TANGY LAMB SHOULDER

Servings: 6   **Cook Time: 5 H 45 Min**   **Prep Time 30 Min**

INGREDIENTS:

- ✓ 1 (5-lb.) bone-in lamb shoulder, trimmed
- ✓ 3-4 tablespoon Moroccan seasoning
- ✓ 2 tablespoon olive oil
- ✓ 1 cup water
- ✓ ¼ cup apple cider vinegar

DIRECTIONS:

- ➢ Set the temperature of the grill to 275°F
- ➢ Preheat with a closed lid for 15 minutes, using charcoal.
- ➢ Coat the lamb shoulder with oil evenly
- ➢ Then rub with Moroccan seasoning generously.
- ➢ Place the lamb shoulder onto the grill
- ➢ Cook for about 45 minutes.
- ➢ In a food-safe spray bottle, mix together vinegar and water.
- ➢ Spray the lamb shoulder with vinegar mixture evenly.
- ➢ Cook for about 4-5 hours, spraying with vinegar mixture after every 20 minutes.
- ➢ Remove the lamb shoulder from the grill
- ➢ Place onto a cutting board for about 20 minutes before slicing.
- ➢ With a sharp knife, cut the lamb shoulder in desired sized slices and serve.

38 CHEESY LAMB BURGERS

Servings: 4   Cook Time: 20 Min   Prep Time 15 Min

INGREDIENTS:

- ✓ 2 lb. ground lamb
- ✓ 1 C. Parmigiano-Reggiano cheese, grated
- ✓ Salt and black pepper, freshly roasted, to taste

DIRECTIONS:

- ➢ Set the temperature of the grill to 425°F
- ➢ Preheat with a closed lid for 15 minutes.
- ➢ In a bowl, add all ingredients and mix well.
- ➢ Make 4 (¾-inch thick) patties from the mixture.
- ➢ With your thumbs, make a shallow but wide depression in each patty.
- ➢ Arrange the patties onto the grill, depression-side down
- ➢ Cook for about 8 minutes.
- ➢ Flip and cook for about 8-10 minutes.
- ➢ Serve immediately.

39 SMOKED RACK OF LAMB

Servings: 4   Cook Time: 1 H 15 Min   Prep Time 30 Min

INGREDIENTS:

- ✓ 1 rack of lamb rib, membrane removed

FOR THE MARINADE:

- ✓ 1 lemon, juiced
- ✓ 2 teaspoons minced garlic
- ✓ 1 teaspoon salt
- ✓ 1 teaspoon ground black pepper
- ✓ 1 teaspoon dried thyme
- ✓ ¼ cup balsamic vinegar
- ✓ 1 teaspoon dried basil

FOR THE GLAZE:

- ✓ 2 tablespoons soy sauce
- ✓ ¼ cup Dijon mustard
- ✓ 2 tablespoons Worcestershire sauce
- ✓ ¼ cup red wine

DIRECTIONS:

- ➢ Prepare the marinade and for this, take a small bowl
- ➢ Place all the ingredients in it and whisk until combined.
- ➢ Put the rack of lamb into a large plastic bag
- ➢ Pour in marinade, seal it, turn it upside down to coat lamb with the marinade
- ➢ Let it marinate for a minimum of 8 hours in the refrigerator.
- ➢ When ready to cook, switch on the grill
- ➢ Fill the grill hopper with flavored wood pellets
- ➢ Power the grill on by using the control panel, select 'smoke' on the temperature dial
- ➢ (Or set the temperature to 300°F)
- ➢ Let it preheat for a minimum of 5 minutes.
- ➢ Meanwhile, prepare the glaze and for this
- ➢ Take a small bowl, place all of its ingredients in it and whisk until combined.
- ➢ When the grill has preheated, open the lid
- ➢ Place lamb rack on the grill grate
- ➢ Shut the grill and smoke for 15 minutes.
- ➢ Brush with glaze, flip the lamb
- ➢ Then continue smoking for 1 hour and 15 minutes
- ➢ (Until the internal temperature reaches 145°F, basting with the glaze every 30 minutes)
- ➢ When done, transfer lamb rack to a cutting board
- ➢ Let it rest for 15 minutes, cut it into slices, and then serve.

40 GARLIC RACK OF LAMB

Servings: 4 | **Cook Time: 3 H** | **Prep Time 30 Min**

INGREDIENTS:

- ✓ 1 rack of lamb, membrane removed
- ✓ FOR THE MARINADE:
- ✓ 2 teaspoons minced garlic
- ✓ 1 teaspoon dried basil
- ✓ $1/3$ cup cream sherry
- ✓ 1 teaspoon dried oregano
- ✓ $1/3$ cup Marsala wine
- ✓ 1 teaspoon dried rosemary
- ✓ $1/2$ teaspoon ground black pepper
- ✓ $1/3$ cup balsamic vinegar
- ✓ 2 tablespoons olive oil

DIRECTIONS:

- ➤ Prepare the marinade and for this, take a small bowl
- ➤ Place all of its ingredients in it and stir until well combined.
- ➤ Put lamb rack in a large plastic bag, pour in marinade
- ➤ Seal the bag, turn it upside down to coat lamb with the marinade
- ➤ Let it marinate for a minimum of 45 minutes in the refrigerator.
- ➤ When ready to cook, switch on the grill
- ➤ Fill the grill hopper with flavored wood pellets
- ➤ Power the grill on by using the control panel
- ➤ Select 'smoke' on the temperature dial
- ➤ (Or set the temperature to 250°F)
- ➤ Let it preheat for a minimum of 5 minutes.
- ➤ Meanwhile,When the grill has preheated, open the lid
- ➤ Place lamb rack on the grill grate
- ➤ Shut the grill, and smoke for 3 hours
- ➤ (Until the internal temperature reaches 165°F)
- ➤ When done, transfer lamb rack to a cutting board
- ➤ Let it rest for 10 Minutes
- ➤ Then cut into slices and serve.

41 WINE BRAISED LAMB SHANK

Servings: 2 | **Cook Time: 10 H** | **Prep Time 30 Min**

INGREDIENTS:

- ✓ 2 (1¼-lb.) lamb shanks
- ✓ 1-2 cups water
- ✓ ¼ cup brown sugar
- ✓ $1/3$ cup rice wine
- ✓ $1/3$ cup soy sauce
- ✓ 1 tablespoon dark sesame oil
- ✓ 4 (1½x½-inch) orange zest strips
- ✓ 2 (3-inch long) cinnamon sticks
- ✓ 1½ teaspoon Chinese five-spice powder

DIRECTIONS:

- ➤ Set the temperature of the grill to 225-250°F
- ➤ Preheat with a closed lid for 15 minutes, using charcoal and soaked Applewood chips.
- ➤ With a sharp knife, pierce each lamb shank at many places.
- ➤ In a bowl, add all remaining ingredients
- ➤ Mix until sugar is dissolved.
- ➤ In a large foil pan, place the lamb shanks
- ➤ Top with sugar mixture evenly.
- ➤ Place the foil pan onto the grill
- ➤ Cook for about 8-10 hours, flipping after every 30 minutes
- ➤ (If required, add enough water to keep the liquid ½-inch over)
- ➤ Remove from the grill and serve hot.

42 CROWN RACK OF LAMB

Servings: 6   **Cook Time: 30 Min**   **Prep Time 15 Min**

INGREDIENTS:

- ✓ 2 racks of lamb, frenched
- ✓ 1 tablespoon garlic, crushed
- ✓ 1 tablespoon rosemary, finely chopped
- ✓ ¼ cup olive oil
- ✓ 2 feet twine

DIRECTIONS:

- ➢ Rinse the racks with cold water
- ➢ Then pat them dry with a paper towel.
- ➢ Lay the racks on a flat board, then score between each bone, about
- ➢ ¼ inch down.
- ➢ In a mixing bowl, mix garlic, rosemary and oil
- ➢ Then generously brush on the lamb.
- ➢ Take each lamb rack and bend it into a semicircle forming a crown-like shape.
- ➢ Use the twine to wrap the racks about 4 times, starting from the base to the top
- ➢ Make sure you tie the twine tightly to keep the racks together.
- ➢ Preheat the wood pellet to 400-450°F
- ➢ Then place the lamb racks on a baking dish
- ➢ Place the baking dish on the pellet grill.
- ➢ Cook for 10 minutes, then reduce temperature to 300°F
- ➢ Cook for 20 more minutes or until the internal temperature reaches 130°F.
- ➢ Remove the lamb rack from the wood pellet
- ➢ Let rest for 15 minutes.
- ➢ Serve, when hot, with veggies and potatoes. Enjoy.

43 LAMB LEG WITH SALSA

Servings: 6   **Cook Time: 1 H 30 Min**   **Prep Time 30 Min**

INGREDIENTS:

- ✓ 6 cloves of garlic, peeled and sliced
- ✓ 1 leg of lamb
- ✓ Salt and pepper to taste
- ✓ 2 btablespoons fresh rosemary, chopped
- ✓ Olive oil
- ✓ 3 cups salsa

DIRECTIONS:

- ➢ Set the wood pellet grill to high.
- ➢ Preheat for 15 minutes while the lid is closed.
- ➢ Make slits all over the lamb leg.
- ➢ Insert the garlic slices.
- ➢ Drizzle with oil and rub with salt, pepper and rosemary.
- ➢ Marinate for 30 minutes.
- ➢ Set the temperature to 350°F.
- ➢ Cook lamb leg for 1 hour and 30 minutes.
- ➢ Serve with salsa.

44 SIMPLE GRILLED LAMB CHOPS

Servings: 6   **Cook Time: 20 Min**   **Prep Time 15 Min**

INGREDIENTS:

- ✓ ¼ cup white vinegar, distilled
- ✓ 2 tablespoons olive oil
- ✓ 2 tablespoons salt
- ✓ ½ tablespoon black pepper
- ✓ 1 tablespoon minced garlic
- ✓ 1 onion, thinly sliced
- ✓ 2 lb. lamb chops

DIRECTIONS:

- ➢ In a resealable bag, mix vinegar, oil, salt, black pepper
- ➢ Then garlic and sliced onions until all salt has dissolved.
- ➢ Add the lamb and toss until evenly coated
- ➢ Place in a fridge to marinate for 2 hours.
- ➢ Preheat your wood pellet grill
- ➢ Remove the lamb from the resealable bag
- ➢ Leave any onion that is stuck on the meat
- ➢ Use an aluminum foil to cover any exposed bone ends.
- ➢ Grill until the desired doneness is achieved
- ➢ Serve and enjoy when hot.

45 PIT BOSS CHILE LIME CHICKEN

Servings: 1   **Cook Time: 20 Min**   **Prep Time 15 Min**

INGREDIENTS:

- ✓ 1 chicken breast
- ✓ 1 tbsp. oil

- ✓ 1 tbsp. spice ology Chile Lime Seasoning

DIRECTIONS:

- ➢ Preheat your Pit boss to 4000F.
- ➢ Brush the chicken breast with oil
- ➢ Then sprinkle the chile-lime seasoning and salt.
- ➢ Place the chicken breast on the grill

- ➢ Cook for 7 minutes on each side
- ➢ (Or until the internal temperature reaches 1650F)
- ➢ Serve when hot and enjoy.

46 GREEK CHICKEN AND VEGGIE KEBABS

Servings: 4   **Cook Time: 14 Min**   **Prep Time 45 Min**

INGREDIENTS:

- ✓ 2tablespoons plain Greek yogurt
- ✓ ¼ cup extra-virgin olive oil Juice of
- ✓ 4 lemons
- ✓ Grated zest of
- ✓ 1 lemon
- ✓ 4 garlic cloves, minced
- ✓ 2 tablespoons dried oregano
- ✓ 1 teaspoon sea salt
- ✓ ½ teaspoon freshly ground black pepper
- ✓ 1 pound chicken breasts that is boneless and skinless, cut into 2- inch cubes
- ✓ 1 red onion, quartered 1 zucchini, sliced

DIRECTIONS:

- ➢ Whisk in a bowl the Greek yogurt, oil
- ➢ Add lemon juice, zest, garlic, oregano, salt, and pepper until well combined.
- ➢ Place the chicken and half of the marinade into a large resealable plastic bag or container
- ➢ Move the chicken around to coat evenly
- ➢ Refrigerate for at least 30 minutes.
- ➢ Close the hood after inserting the grill grate
- ➢ Start pre-heating for 14 minutes.
- ➢ While the unit is preheating, assemble the kebabs by threading the chicken on the skewers

- ➢ Alternating with the red onion and zucchini
- ➢ Ensure the ingredients are pushed almost completely down to the end of the skewers.
- ➢ Place the skewers on the Grill Grate
- ➢ (When the device beeps to signal that it has preheated)
- ➢ Close hood and cook for 10 to 14 minutes
- ➢ Occasionally basting the kebabs with the remaining marinade while cooking.
- ➢ The chicken is now ready when the internal temperature of the meat exceeds 165 ° F.

48 PIT BOSS GRILLED BUFFALO CHICKEN

Servings: 6   **Cook Time: 10 Min**   **Prep Time 15 Min**

INGREDIENTS:

- ✓ 5 chicken breasts, boneless and skinless
- ✓ 2 tbsp. homemade Grill rub
- ✓ 1 cup homemade Cholula Buffalo sauce

DIRECTIONS:

- ➤ Preheat the Pit boss to 4000F.
- ➤ Slice the chicken breast lengthwise into strips
- ➤ Season the slices with Grill rub.
- ➤ Place the chicken slices on the grill
- ➤ Paint both sides with buffalo sauce.
- ➤ Cook for 4 minutes with the lid closed
- ➤ Flip the breasts, paint again with sauce
- ➤ Cook until the internal temperature reaches 1650F.
- ➤ Remove the chicken from the
- ➤ Pit boss and serve when warm.

49 PIT BOSS SHEET PAN CHICKEN FAJITAS

Servings: 10   **Cook Time: 10 Min**   **Prep Time 10 Min**

INGREDIENTS:

- ✓ 1 lb. chicken breast 1 onion, sliced.
- ✓ 1 red bell pepper seeded and sliced.
- ✓ 1 orange-red bell pepper seeded and sliced
- ✓ 1 tbsp. salt
- ✓ 1/2 tbsp. onion powder
- ✓ 1/2 tbsp. granulated garlic
- ✓ 2 tbsp. Spice ologist Chile Margarita Seasoning
- ✓ 2 tbsp. oil

DIRECTIONS:

- ➤ Preheat the Pit boss to 4500F and line a baking sheet with parchment paper.
- ➤ In a mixing bowl, combine seasonings and oil
- ➤ Then toss with the peppers and chicken.
- ➤ Place the baking sheet in the Pit boss
- ➤ Let heat for 10 minutes with the lid closed.
- ➤ Open the lid and place the veggies and the chicken in a single layer. Close the lid and cook for 10 minutes or until the chicken is no longer pink.
- ➤ Serve with warm tortillas and top with your favorite toppings.

50 PIT BOSS ASIAN MISO CHICKEN WINGS

Servings: 6   **Cook Time: 25 Min**   **Prep Time 15 Min**

INGREDIENTS:

- ✓ 2 lb. chicken wings
- ✓ 3/4 cup soy
- ✓ 1/2 cup pineapple juice
- ✓ 1 tbsp. sriracha
- ✓ 1/8 cup miso
- ✓ 1/8 cup gochujang
- ✓ 1/2 cup water
- ✓ 1/2 cup oil
- ✓ Togarashi

DIRECTIONS:

- ➤ Preheat the Pit boss to 3750F
- ➤ Combine all the ingredients except togarashi in a zip lock bag
- ➤ Toss until the chicken wings are well coated
- ➤ Refrigerate for 12 hours.
- ➤ Pace the wings on the grill grates and close the lid
- ➤ Cook for 25 minutes or until the internal temperature reaches 1650F.
- ➤ Remove the wings from the Pit boss and sprinkle Togarashi.
- ➤ Serve when hot and enjoy.

51 LEMON AND FRESH HERB GRILLED CHICKEN THIGHS

Servings: 4   **Cook Time: 13 Min**   **Prep Time 40 Min**

INGREDIENTS:

- ✓ Grated zest of 2 lemons Juice of
- ✓ 2 lemons
- ✓ 2 sprigs fresh rosemary, leaves finely chopped
- ✓ 3 sprigs fresh sage, leaves finely chopped
- ✓ 2 garlic cloves, minced
- ✓ ¼ teaspoon red pepper flakes
- ✓ ¼ cup canola oil
- ✓ Sea salt
- ✓ 4 (4-to 7-ounce) boneless chicken thighs

DIRECTIONS:

- ➢ Toss the lemon zest and juice, rosemary
- ➢ Add sage, garlic, red pepper flakes, and oil together in a small cup. With salt, season.
- ➢ Place the chicken and lemon-herb mixture in a large resealable plastic bag or container
- ➢ Toss to coat evenly
- ➢ Refrigerate the chicken for at least 30 minutes.
- ➢ Insert and close the hood with the Grill Grate
- ➢ Choose GRILL, set the heat to HIGH, and set the time to 13 minutes
- ➢ To commence preheating, click START/STOP.
- ➢ Place the chicken on the Grill Grate when the device beeps to signal that it has preheated
- ➢ For 10 to 13 minutes, close the hood and cook.
- ➢ When the internal temperature of the meat reaches 165F, that is when cooking is complete.

52 ZESTY GARLIC GRILLED CHICKEN

Servings: 4   **Cook Time: 18 Min**   **Prep Time 40 Min**

INGREDIENTS:

- ✓ 1½ tablespoons extra-virgin olive oil
- ✓ 3 garlic cloves, minced
- ✓ ¼ teaspoon ground cumin
- ✓ Sea salt
- ✓ Freshly ground black pepper
- ✓ Grated zest of 1 lime
- ✓ Juice of 1 lime
- ✓ 4 boneless, skinless chicken breasts

DIRECTIONS:

- ➢ Stir the oil, garlic, cumin, salt, pepper, zest, and lime juice together in a large shallow cup
- ➢ Attach the breasts of the chicken and coat well
- ➢ Cover and marinate for 30 minutes in the refrigerator.
- ➢ Insert and close the hood with the Grill Grate
- ➢ Choose a GRILL, set the MEDIUM temperature
- ➢ Set the time to 18 minutes
- ➢ To commence preheating, click START/STOP.
- ➢ When the unit has beeped to signify it has preheated
- ➢ Place the chicken breasts on the Grill Grate
- ➢ Close the hood and cook for 7 minutes
- ➢ After 7 minutes, flip the chicken, close the hood
- ➢ Cook for an additional 7 minutes.
- ➢ Check the chicken for doneness. If needed, cook up to 4 minutes more
- ➢ When the internal temperature of the chicken meat reaches 165F, that is when cooking is complete.
- ➢ Remove from the grill, and position for 5 minutes on a cutting board or platter to rest. Just serve.

53 HONEY-SRIRACHA GRILLED CHICKEN THIGHS

Servings: 4   **Cook Time: 17 Min**   **Prep Time 40 Min**

INGREDIENTS:

- ✓ 1 cup sriracha Juice of
- ✓ 2 lemons
- ✓ ¼ cup honey
- ✓ 4 bone-in chicken thighs

DIRECTIONS:

- ➢ Place the sriracha, lemon juice, and honey in a large resealable plastic bag or container
- ➢ Add the chicken thighs and toss to coat evenly
- ➢ Refrigerate for 30 minutes.
- ➢ Insert and close the hood with the Grill Grate
- ➢ Pre-heat for fourteen minutes.
- ➢ Place the chicken thighs onto the Grill Grate after pre-heating
- ➢ Gently press them down to maximize grill marks
- ➢ Close the hood and cook for 7 minutes.
- ➢ After 7 minutes, flip the chicken thighs using tongs
- ➢ Close the hood and cook for 7 minutes more.
- ➢ Cooking is complete when, on a food thermometer, the internal temperature of the meat reaches at least 165 °F
- ➢ Close the hood if necessary and continue cooking for an additional 2 to 3 minutes.
- ➢ When the cooking is finished, remove the chicken from the grill and let it rest for 5 minutes prior to serving.

54 MAPLE-GLAZED CHICKEN WINGS

Servings: 4   **Cook Time: 14 Min**   **Prep Time 15 Min**

INGREDIENTS:

- ✓ 1 cup maple syrup
- ✓ 1/3 cup soy sauce
- ✓ ¼ cup teriyaki sauce
- ✓ 3 garlic cloves, minced
- ✓ 2 teaspoons garlic powder
- ✓ 2 teaspoons onion powder
- ✓ 1 teaspoon freshly ground black pepper
- ✓ 2 pounds bone-in chicken wings (drumettes and flats)

DIRECTIONS:

- ➢ Insert and close the hood with the Grill Grate
- ➢ Choose a GRILL, set the MEDIUM temperature, and set the time to 14 minutes
- ➢ To commence preheating, click START/STOP.
- ➢ Meanwhile, in a large bowl, whisk together the maple
- ➢ Then syrup, soy sauce, teriyaki sauce, garlic, garlic powder, onion powder, and black pepper
- ➢ Add the wings, and use tongs to toss and coat.
- ➢ When the unit has beeped to signify it has preheated
- ➢ Place the chicken wings on the Grill Grate
- ➢ Close the hood and cook for 5 minutes
- ➢ After 5 minutes, flip the wings, close the hood
- ➢ Cook for an additional 5 minutes.
- ➢ Check the wings for doneness
- ➢ Cooking is complete when, on a food thermometer, the internal temperature of the meat reaches at least 165 °F
- ➢ If needed, cook for up to 4 minutes more.
- ➢ Remove from the grill and serve.

55 GRILLED MARINATED CHICKEN

Servings: 4   **Cook Time: 26 Min**   **Prep T.5 Min (2 H Marinate)**

INGREDIENTS:

- ✓ 1/2 cup soy sauce
- ✓ 1/4 cup rice wine
- ✓ 1 1/2 Tbsp. finely chopped onion
- ✓ 5 skinless, boneless chicken breasts, thinly sliced
- ✓ 1 Tbsp. sesame oil for brushing the chicken on both sides before grilling
- ✓ 1/2 cup beans sprouts

- ✓ 2 medium sized mushrooms, sliced
- ✓ 1 small daikon, julienned
- ✓ 1 small carrot, julienned salt and pepper to taste
- ✓ 2 eggs
- ✓ 3 pcs small green onions cut into pieces
- ✓ 4-6 lettuce leaves
- ✓ 4-6 burger buns, toasted

DIRECTIONS:

- ➤ In a large bowl, mix the soy sauce, rice wine, onion and sesame oil
- ➤ Add the chicken breasts and marinate for at least 3 hours.
- ➤ Drain excess marinade from the chicken.
- ➤ Grill on medium heat until done
- ➤ Mix the sprouts with mushrooms, daikon and carrots in a small bowl
- ➤ Season with salt & pepper to taste while tossing gently with a spatula or spoon
- ➤ Slice burgers in half

- ➤ Beat the eggs in a shallow bowl
- ➤ Paint both sides of the toasted burger buns with beaten eggs
- ➤ Grill both side of buns on medium heat until slightly browned (approximately 3 minutes)
- ➤ Assemble burgers: Place lettuce, cole slaw, longaniza and 2 halves of egg on toasted burger bun
- ➤ Arrange mushroom paste mixture and chicken/marinade over the cole slaw
- ➤ Put last half of egg over the longaniza

56 SPICY BARBECUE CHICKEN DRUMSTICKS

Servings: 4   **Cook Time: 20 Min**   **Prep Time 10 Min**

INGREDIENTS:

- ✓ 2 cups barbecue sauce
- ✓ Juice of 1 lime
- ✓ 2 tablespoons honey
- ✓ 1 tablespoon hot sauce
- ✓ Sea salt
- ✓ Freshly ground black pepper
- ✓ 1 pound chicken drumsticks

DIRECTIONS:

- ➤ In a large bowl, combine the barbecue sauce, lime juice, honey, and hot sauce
- ➤ Season with salt and pepper. Set aside ½ cup of the sauce
- ➤ Add the drumsticks to the bowl, and toss until evenly coated.
- ➤ Insert the Grill Grate and close the hood
- ➤ Select GRILL, set the temperature to MEDIUM, and set the time to 20 minutes
- ➤ Select START/STOP to begin preheating.

- ➤ When the unit beeps to signify it has preheated
- ➤ Place the drumsticks on the Grill Grate
- ➤ Close the hood and cook for 18 minutes, basting often during cooking.
- ➤ Cooking is complete when the internal temperature of the meat reaches at least 165°F on a food thermometer
- ➤ If necessary, close the hood and continue cooking for 2 minutes more.

57 GRILLED CHICKEN PICCATA

Servings: 2   **Cook Time: 22 Min**   **Prep Time 5 Min**

INGREDIENTS:

- ✓ 2 to 3 pounds chicken (I'm using chicken thighs)
- ✓ Salt and pepper
- ✓ 1/4 cup extra-virgin olive oil 1 lemon, juice of
- ✓ 1/4 cup capers
- ✓ Optional: fresh chopped herbs, like parsley or rosemary.

DIRECTIONS:

- ➤ Rinse chicken, pat dry then season with salt and pepper.
- ➤ Place on a medium to high sided grill
- ➤ Cook until done, turning as needed
- ➤ When done, let rest for 5 minutes before slicing*.
- ➤ Meanwhile, place a large non-stick frying pan on medium high heat
- ➤ Add the oil and the capers and cook for 1 minute or so, stirring frequently.
- ➤ Scrape up all the good bits from the bottom of the pan so you don't lose any of that flavor!
- ➤ Add lemon juice, stir then reduce heat to low.

58 GRILLED CHICKEN CUTLETS

Servings: 4   **Cook Time: 10 Min**   **Prep Time 20 Min**

INGREDIENTS:

- ✓ 3 medium cloves garlic, minced (about 1 tablespoon)
- ✓ 3 tablespoons minced fresh rosemary
- ✓ 2 tablespoons fresh juice from
- ✓ 2 lemons
- ✓ 2 teaspoons kosher salt
- ✓ 1 teaspoon freshly ground black pepper 1/4 cup olive oil
- ✓ 4 chicken cutlets, about 1 ½ pounds total weight, halved crosswise if necessary to make even thicknesses

DIRECTIONS:

- ➤ In a small bowl, stir together the garlic, rosemary, lemon juice, salt and pepper
- ➤ Gradually whisk in the oil until blended.
- ➤ Place chicken pieces between 2 pieces of plastic wrap
- ➤ Pound to an even thickness using a meat mallet or small heavy skillet.
- ➤ In a large zip-top plastic bag, combine the chicken pieces and marinade. Seal and toss to coat
- ➤ Let stand at room temperature for 15 minutes, turning once.
- ➤ Marinate longer if possible, turning occasionally.
- ➤ Prepare the grill for direct grilling over medium-high heat (350° to 450°)
- ➤ Meanwhile, oil the grill rack or spray with nonstick spray
- ➤ Lightly grease the chicken pieces on both sides with oil from a spray bottle before grilling.
- ➤ Prepare the chicken on the grill rack
- ➤ Brush with any remaining marinade, and turn occasionally
- ➤ Grill until done, turning once
- ➤ Brush with more of the marinade as necessary to prevent sticking and drying out.

59 GRILLED HALIBUT

Servings: 4   **Cook Time: 30 Min**   **Prep Time 10 Min**

INGREDIENTS:
- ✓ 1 pound fresh halibut filet (cut into 4 equal sizes)
- ✓ 1 tbsp. fresh lemon juice
- ✓ 2 garlic cloves (minced)
- ✓ 2 tsp soy sauce
- ✓ ½ tsp ground black pepper
- ✓ ½ tsp onion powder
- ✓ 2 tbsp. honey
- ✓ ½ tsp oregano
- ✓ 1 tsp dried basil
- ✓ 2 tbsp. butter (melted)
- ✓ Maple syrup for serving.

DIRECTIONS:
- ➤ Combine the lemon juice, honey, soy sauce
- ➤ Add onion powder, oregano, dried basil, pepper, and garlic.
- ➤ Brush the halibut filets generously with the filet the mixture
- ➤ Wrap the filets with aluminum foil and refrigerate for 4 hours.
- ➤ Remove the filets from the refrigerator
- ➤ Let them sit for about 2 hours, or until they are at room temperature.
- ➤ Activate your wood pellet grill on smoke
- ➤ Leave the lid opened for 5 minutes or until fire starts.
- ➤ The lid must not be opened for it to be preheated and reach 275°F 15 minutes, using fruit wood pellets.
- ➤ Place the halibut filets directly on the grill grate
- ➤ Smoke for 30 minutes.
- ➤ Remove the filets from the grill
- ➤ Let them rest for 10 minutes.
- ➤ Serve and top with maple syrup to taste.

60 GRILLED SHRIMP

Servings: 8   **Cook Time: 8 Min**   **Prep Time 20 Min**

INGREDIENTS:
- ✓ 1 pound raw shrimp (peeled and deveined)
- ✓ ¼ cup extra virgin olive oil
- ✓ ½ tsp paprika
- ✓ ½ tsp red pepper flakes
- ✓ 2 garlic cloves (minced)
- ✓ 1 tsp cumin
- ✓ 1 lemon (juiced)
- ✓ 1 tsp kosher salt
- ✓ 1 tbsp. chili paste
- ✓ Bamboo or wooden skewers (soaked for 30 minutes, at least)

DIRECTIONS:
- ➤ Combine the pepper flakes, cumin, lemon, salt, chili, paprika, garlic and olive oil
- ➤ Add the shrimp and toss to combine.
- ➤ Transfer the shrimp and marinade into a zip-lock bag and refrigerate for 4 hours.
- ➤ Let shrimp rest in room temperature after pulling it out from marinade.
- ➤ Start your grill on smoke, leaving the lid opened for 5 minutes
- ➤ (Or until fire starts)
- ➤ Use hickory wood pellet.
- ➤ Keep lid unopened and preheat the grill to "high" for 15 minutes.
- ➤ Thread shrimps onto skewers
- ➤ Arrange the skewers on the grill grate.
- ➤ Smoke shrimps for 8 minutes, 4 minutes per side.
- ➤ Serve and enjoy.

61 GRILLED COYSTER IN SHELLS

Servings: 4 **Cook Time: 8 Min** **Prep Time 25 Min**

INGREDIENTS:
- ✓ 12 medium oysters
- ✓ 1 tsp oregano
- ✓ 1 lemon (juiced)
- ✓ 1 tsp freshly ground black pepper.
- ✓ 6 tbsp. unsalted butter (melted)
- ✓ 1 tsp salt or more to taste
- ✓ 2 garlic cloves (minced)
- ✓ ½ tbsp. grated parmesan cheese
- ✓ 2 tbsp. freshly chopped parsley

DIRECTIONS:
- ➤ Remove dirt.
- ➤ Open the shell completely. Discard the top shell.
- ➤ Gently run the knife under the oyster to loosen the oyster foot from the bottom shell.
- ➤ Repeat step 2 and 3 for the remaining oysters.
- ➤ Combine melted butter, lemon, pepper, salt, garlic, and oregano in a mixing bowl.
- ➤ Pour ½ to 1 tsp of the butter mixture on each oyster.
- ➤ Start your wood pellet grill on smoke
- ➤ Leave the lid opened for 5 minutes, or until fire starts.
- ➤ Keep lid unopened to preheat in the set "HIGH" with lid closed for 15 minutes.
- ➤ Gently arrange the oysters onto the grill grate.
- ➤ Grill oyster for 6 to 8 minutes
- ➤ (Or until the oyster juice is bubbling and the oyster is plump)
- ➤ Remove oysters from heat
- ➤ Serve and top with grated parmesan and chopped parsley.

62 CAJUN SMOKED CATFISH

Servings: 4 **Cook Time: 2 H** **Prep Time 15 Min**

INGREDIENTS:
- ✓ 4 catfish fillets (5 ounces each)
- ✓ ½ cup Cajun seasoning
- ✓ 1 tsp ground black pepper.
- ✓ 1 tbsp. smoked paprika.
- ✓ 1 /4 tsp cayenne pepper
- ✓ 1 tsp hot sauce
- ✓ 1 tsp granulated garlic
- ✓ 1 tsp onion powder
- ✓ 1 tsp thyme
- ✓ 1 tsp salt or more to taste
- ✓ 2 tbsp. chopped fresh parsley.

DIRECTIONS:
- ➤ Pour water into the bottom of a square or rectangular dish
- ➤ Add 4 tbsp. salt
- ➤ Arrange the catfish fillets into the dish
- ➤ Cover the dish and refrigerate for 3 to 4 hours.
- ➤ Combine the paprika, cayenne, hot sauce
- ➤ Then onion, salt, thyme, garlic,pepper, and Cajun seasoning in a mixing bowl.
- ➤ Remove the fish from the dish and let it sit for a few minutes
- ➤ (Or until it is at room temperature)
- ➤ Pat the fish fillets dry with a paper towel.
- ➤ Rub the seasoning mixture over each fillet generously.
- ➤ Start your grill on smoke, leaving the lid opened for 5 minutes, or until fire starts.
- ➤ Keep lid unopened and preheat to 200°F, using mesquite hardwood pellets.
- ➤ Arrange the fish fillets onto the grill grate and close the grill
- ➤ Cook for about 2 hours, or until the fish is flaky.
- ➤ Remove the fillets from the grill
- ➤ Let the fillets rest for a few minutes to cool.
- ➤ Serve and garnish with chopped fresh parsley.

63 SMOKED SCALLOPS

Servings: 6   **Cook Time: 15 Min**   **Prep Time 10 Min**

INGREDIENTS:
- ✓ 2 pounds sea scallops
- ✓ 4 tbsp. salted butter
- ✓ 2 tbsp. lemon juice
- ✓ ½ tsp ground black pepper
- ✓ 1 garlic clove (minced)
- ✓ 1 kosher tsp salt
- ✓ 1 tsp freshly chopped tarragon

DIRECTIONS:
- ➢ Let the scallops dry using paper towels
- ➢ Drizzle all sides with salt and pepper to season.
- ➢ Place you are a cast iron pan in your grill
- ➢ Preheat the grill to 400°F with lid closed for 15 minutes.
- ➢ Combine the butter and garlic in hot cast iron pan
- ➢ Add the scallops and stir. Close grill lid and cook for 8 minutes.
- ➢ Flip the scallops and cook for an additional 7 minutes.
- ➢ Remove the scallop from heat and let it rest for a few minutes.
- ➢ Stir in the chopped tarragon. Serve and top with lemon juice.

64 PIT BOSS SALMON WITH TOGARASHI

Servings: 3   **Cook Time: 20 Min**   **Prep Time 5 Min**

INGREDIENTS:
- ✓ One salmon fillet
- ✓ 1/4 cup olive oil
- ✓ 1/2 tbsp kosher salt
- ✓ 1 tbsp Togarashi seasoning

DIRECTIONS:
- ➢ Preheat your Pit boss to 4000F.
- ➢ Place the salmon on a sheet lined with non-stick foil with the skin side down.
- ➢ Rub the oil into the meat, then sprinkle salt and Togarashi.
- ➢ Place the salmon on the grill and cook for 20 minutes
- ➢ (Or until the internal temperature reaches 1450 F with the lid closed)
- ➢ Remove from the Pit boss and serve when hot.

65 GRILLED TRAGER ROCKFISH

Servings: 6   **Cook Time: 20 Min**   **Prep Time 10 Min**

INGREDIENTS:
- ✓ Six rockfish fillets
- ✓ One lemon, sliced.
- ✓ 3/4 tbsp salt
- ✓ 1 tbsp fresh dill, chopped
- ✓ 1/2 tbsp garlic powder
- ✓ 1/2 tbsp onion powder
- ✓ 6 tbsp butter

DIRECTIONS:
- ➢ Preheat your Pit boss to 4000F.
- ➢ Season the fish with salt, dill, garlic, and onion powder on both sides
- ➢ Then place it in a baking dish.
- ➢ Place a pat of butter and a lemon slice on each fillet
- ➢ Place the baking dish in the Pit boss and close the lid.
- ➢ Cook for 20 minutes or until the fish is no longer translucent and is flaky.
- ➢ Remove from Pit boss and let rest before serving.

66 PIT BOSS GRILLED LINGCOD

Servings: 6   **Cook Time: 15 Min**   **Prep Time 10 Min**

INGREDIENTS:
- ✓ 2 lb. lingcod fillets
- ✓ 1/2 tbsp salt
- ✓ 1/2 tbsp white pepper
- ✓ 1/4 tbsp cayenne pepper
- ✓ Lemon wedges

DIRECTIONS:
- ➤ Preheat your Pit boss to 375F.
- ➤ Place the lingcod on a parchment paper or a grill mat.
- ➤ Season the fish with salt, pepper, and top with lemon wedges.
- ➤ Cook the fish for 15 minutes

67 GRILLED SHRIMP KABOBS

Servings: 4   **Cook Time: 10 Min**   **Prep Time 5 Min**

INGREDIENTS:
- ✓ 1 lb. colossal shrimp peeled and deveined.
- ✓ 2 tbsp. oil
- ✓ 1/2 tbsp. garlic salt
- ✓ 1/2 tbsp. salt
- ✓ 1/8 tbsp. pepper
- ✓ Six skewers

DIRECTIONS:
- ➤ Preheat your Pit boss to 3750F.
- ➤ Pat the shrimp dry with a paper towel.
- ➤ In a mixing bowl, mix oil, garlic salt, salt, and pepper.
- ➤ Toss the shrimp in the mixture until well coated.
- ➤ Skewer the shrimps and cook in the Pit boss with the lid closed for 4 minutes.
- ➤ Open the lid, flip the skewers, cook for another 4 minutes
- ➤ (Or wait until the shrimp is pink and the flesh is opaque)
- ➤ Serve.

68 GRILLED SWEET BACON-WRAPPED SHRIMP

Servings: 12   **Cook Time: 10 Min**   **Prep Time 20 Min**

INGREDIENTS:
- ✓ 1 lb. raw shrimp
- ✓ 1/2 tbsp salt
- ✓ 1/4 tbsp garlic powder
- ✓ 1 lb. bacon cut into halves.

DIRECTIONS:
- ➤ Preheat your Pit boss to 3500F.
- ➤ Remove the shells and tails from the shrimp
- ➤ Then pat them dry with the paper towels.
- ➤ Sprinkle salt and garlic on the shrimp
- ➤ At this point wrap with bacon and secure with a toothpick.
- ➤ Place the shrimps on a baking rack greased with cooking spray.
- ➤ Cook for 10 minutes, flip and cook for another 10 minutes
- ➤ (Or until the bacon is crisp enough)
- ➤ Remove from the Pit boss and serve.

69 GRILLED SPOT PRAWN SKEWERS

Servings: 6 **Cook Time: 10 Min** **Prep Time 10 Min**

INGREDIENTS:

- ✓ 1 lb. spot prawns
- ✓ 2 tbsp oil
- ✓ Salt and pepper to taste

DIRECTIONS:

- ➢ Preheat your Pit boss to 4000F.
- ➢ Skewer your prawns with soaked skewers
- ➢ Then generously sprinkle with oil, salt, and pepper.
- ➢ Place the skewers on the grill
- ➢ Cook with the lid closed for 5 minutes on each side.
- ➢ Remove the skewers and serve when hot.

70 GRILLED BACON-WRAPPED SCALLOPS

Servings: 8 **Cook Time: 20 Min** **Prep Time 15 Min**

INGREDIENTS:

- ✓ 1 lb. sea scallops
- ✓ 1/2 lb. bacon
- ✓ Sea salt

DIRECTIONS:

- ➢ Preheat your Pit boss to 3750F.
- ➢ Pat dries the scallops with a towel
- ➢ Then wrap them with a piece of bacon and secure with a toothpick.
- ➢ Lay the scallops on the grill with the bacon side down
- ➢ Close the lid and cook for 5 minutes on each side.
- ➢ Keep the scallops on the bacon side so that you will not get grill marks on the scallops.
- ➢ Serve and enjoy.

71 GRILLED LOBSTER TAIL

Servings: 2 **Cook Time: 15 Min** **Prep Time 10 Min**

INGREDIENTS:

- ✓ 10 oz lobster tail
- ✓ 1/4 tbsp old bay seasoning
- ✓ 1/4 tbsp Himalayan salt
- ✓ 2 tbsp butter, melted.
- ✓ 1 tbsp fresh parsley, chopped.

DIRECTIONS:

- ➢ Preheat your Pit boss to 4500F.
- ➢ Slice the tail down the middle
- ➢ Then season it with bay seasoning and salt.
- ➢ Place the tails directly on the grill with the meat side down
- ➢ Grill for 15 minutes or until the internal temperature reaches 1400F.
- ➢ Remove from the Pit boss and drizzle with butter.
- ➢ Serve when hot garnished with parsley.

72 GRILLED STUFFED TOMATOES

Servings: 2   **Cook Time: 14 Min**   **Prep Time 15 Min**

INGREDIENTS:

- ✓ 1 large tomatoes
- ✓ ½ cup broccoli, chopped finely
- ✓ ½ cup cheddar cheese, shredded
- ✓ 1 tablespoon unsalted butter, melted
- ✓ ½ teaspoon dried thyme, crushed

DIRECTIONS:

- ➢ Carefully cut the top of each tomato and scoop out pulp and seeds.
- ➢ In a bowl, place the chopped broccoli and cheese and mix.
- ➢ Stuff each tomato with broccoli mixture evenly.
- ➢ Arrange the "Crisper Basket" in the pot of Griller.
- ➢ Close the Griller with lid and select "Air Crisp".
- ➢ Set the temperature to 355 degrees F to preheat.
- ➢ Press "Start/Stop" to begin preheating.
- ➢ When the display shows
- ➢ Add Food opens the lid and places the tomatoes into the Crisper Basket.
- ➢ Drizzle the tomatoes with the butter.
- ➢ Close the Griller with lid and set the time for 15 minutes.
- ➢ Press "Start/Stop" to begin cooking.
- ➢ When the cooking time is completed, press "Start/Stop" to stop cooking and open the lid.
- ➢ Serve with the garnishing of thyme.

73 GRILLED CHEESY SPINACH

Servings: 4   **Cook Time: 15 Min**   **Prep Time 15 Min**

INGREDIENTS:

- ✓ 1 pound fresh spinach, chopped
- ✓ 4 tablespoons butter, melted
- ✓ Salt and ground black pepper, as required
- ✓ 1 cup feta cheese, crumbled
- ✓ 1 teaspoon fresh lemon zest, grated

DIRECTIONS:

- ➢ In a bowl, add the spinach, butter, salt and black pepper and mix well.
- ➢ Arrange the "Crisper Basket" in the pot of Griller.
- ➢ Close the Griller with lid and select "Air Crisp".
- ➢ Set the temperature to 340 degrees F to preheat.
- ➢ Press "Start/Stop" to begin preheating.
- ➢ When the display shows
- ➢ Add Food opens the lid
- ➢ Place the spinach mixture into the Crisper Basket.
- ➢ Close the Griller with lid and set the time for 15 minutes.
- ➢ Press "Start/Stop" to begin cooking.
- ➢ When the cooking time is completed
- ➢ Press "Start/Stop" to stop cooking and open the lid.
- ➢ Immediately transfer the spinach mixture into a bowl.
- ➢ Add the cheese and lemon zest and stir to combine.
- ➢ Serve hot.

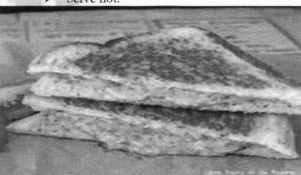

74 POTATO GRATIN

Servings: 4 **Cook Time: 20 Min** **Prep Time 15 Min**

INGREDIENTS:
- ✓ 1 large potatoes, sliced thinly
- ✓ 5½ tablespoons cream
- ✓ 2 eggs
- ✓ 1 tablespoon plain flour
- ✓ ½ cup cheddar cheese, grated

DIRECTIONS:
- ➤ Arrange the "Crisper Basket" in the pot of Griller.
- ➤ Close the Griller with lid and select "Air Crisp".
- ➤ Set the temperature to 355 degrees F to preheat.
- ➤ Press "Start/Stop" to begin preheating.
- ➤ When the display shows
- ➤ Add Food opens the lid and place the potato slices into the Crisper Basket.
- ➤ Close the Griller with lid and set the time for 10 minutes.
- ➤ Press "Start/Stop" to begin cooking.
- ➤ Meanwhile, in a bowl, add cream, eggs and flour
- ➤ mix until a thick sauce form.
- ➤ When the cooking time is completed, press "Start/Stop" to stop cooking and open the lid.

- ➤ Remove the potato slices from the "Crisper Basket".
- ➤ Divide the potato slices in 4 ramekins evenly
- ➤ top with the egg mixture evenly, followed by the cheese.
- ➤ Arrange the ramekins into the "Crisper Basket".
- ➤ Close the Griller with lid and select "Air Crisp".
- ➤ Set the temperature to 390 degrees F for 10 minutes.
- ➤ Press "Start/Stop" to begin cooking.
- ➤ When the cooking time is completed, press "Start/Stop" to stop cooking and open the lid.
- ➤ Serve warm.

75 GLAZED VEGGIES

Servings: 4 **Cook Time: 25 Min** **Prep Time 15 Min**

INGREDIENTS:
- ✓ 1 ounces cherry tomatoes
- ✓ 2 large zucchinis, chopped
- ✓ 2 green bell peppers, seeded and chopped
- ✓ 6 tablespoons olive oil, divided
- ✓ 2 tablespoons honey
- ✓ 1 teaspoon Dijon mustard
- ✓ 1 teaspoon dried herbs
- ✓ 1 teaspoon garlic paste
- ✓ Salt, as required

DIRECTIONS:
- ➤ In a parchment paper-lined baking pan, place the vegetables
- ➤ Drizzle with 3 tablespoons of oil.
- ➤ Arrange the "Crisper Basket" in the pot of Griller.
- ➤ Close the Griller with lid and select "Air Crisp".
- ➤ Set the temperature to 350 degrees F to preheat.
- ➤ Press "Start/Stop" to begin preheating.
- ➤ When the display shows "Add Food" open the lid
- ➤ Places the pan into the "Crisper Basket".
- ➤ Close the Griller with lid and set the time for 20 minutes.
- ➤ Press "Start/Stop" to begin cooking.
- ➤ Meanwhile, in a bowl, add the remaining oil, honey

- ➤ Then mustard, herbs, garlic, salt, and black pepper and mix well.
- ➤ When the cooking time is completed, press "Start/Stop" to stop cooking and open the lid.
- ➤ Stir the honey mixture with vegetable mixture.
- ➤ Again, arrange the pan into the "Crisper Basket".
- ➤ Close the Griller with lid and select "Air Crisp".
- ➤ Set the temperature to 392 degrees F for 5 minutes.
- ➤ Press "Start/Stop" to begin cooking.
- ➤ When the cooking time is completed, press "Start/Stop" to stop cooking and open the lid.
- ➤ Serve immediately.

76 TOFU WITH ORANGE SAUCE

Servings: 4   **Cook Time: 20 Min**   **Prep Time 15 Min**

INGREDIENTS:

FOR TOFU:

✓ 1 pound extra-firm tofu, pressed and cubed
✓ 1 tablespoon cornstarch

FOR SAUCE:

✓ ½ cup water
✓ 1/3 cup fresh orange juice
✓ 1 tablespoon honey
✓ 1 teaspoon orange zest, grated

✓ 1 tablespoon tamari

✓ 1 teaspoon garlic, minced
✓ 1 teaspoon fresh ginger, minced
✓ 2 teaspoons cornstarch
✓ ¼ teaspoon red pepper flakes, crushed

DIRECTIONS:

➢ In a bowl, add the tofu, cornstarch, and tamari and toss to coat well.
➢ Set the tofu aside to marinate for at least 15 minutes.
➢ Arrange the greased "Crisper Basket" in the pot of Griller.
➢ Close the Griller with lid and select "Air Crisp".
➢ Set the temperature to 390 degrees F to preheat.
➢ Press "Start/Stop" to begin preheating.
➢ When the display shows "Add Food" opens the lid and place the tofu cubes into the "Crisper Basket".

➢ Close the Griller with lid and set the time for 10 minutes.
➢ Press "Start/Stop" to begin cooking.
➢ Meanwhile, for the sauce: in a small pan, add all the ingredients over medium-high heat and bring to a boil, stirring continuously.
➢ When the cooking time is completed, press "Start/Stop" to stop cooking and open the lid.
➢ Transfer the tofu into a serving bowl.
➢ Add the sauce and gently stir to combine.
➢ Serve immediately.

77 ROASTED CASHEWS

Servings: 6   **Cook Time: 5 Min**   **Prep Time 5 Min**

INGREDIENTS:

✓ 1½ cups raw cashew nuts
✓ 1 teaspoon butter, melted

✓ Salt and freshly ground black pepper, as needed

DIRECTIONS:

➢ In a bowl, add all the ingredients and toss to coat well.
➢ Arrange the "Crisper Basket" in the pot of Griller.
➢ Close the Griller with lid and select "Air Crisp".
➢ Set the temperature to 355 degrees F to preheat.
➢ Press "Start/Stop" to begin preheating.
➢ When the display shows "Add Food" open the lid and place the cashews into the "Crisper Basket".

➢ Close the Griller with lid and set the time for 5 minutes.
➢ Press "Start/Stop" to begin cooking.
➢ Shake the cashews once halfway through.
➢ When the cooking time is completed, press "Start/Stop" to stop cooking and open the lid.
➢ Transfer the cashews onto a platter and set aside to cool before serving.

78 POTATO CROQUETTES

Servings: 4   **Cook Time: 23 Min**   **Prep Time 15 Min**

INGREDIENTS:

- ✓ 1 medium Russet potatoes, peeled and cubed
- ✓ 2 tablespoons all-purpose flour
- ✓ ½ cup Parmesan cheese, grated
- ✓ 1 egg yolk
- ✓ 2 tablespoons chives, minced
- ✓ Pinch of ground nutmeg
- ✓ Salt and ground black pepper, as required
- ✓ 2 eggs
- ✓ ½ cup breadcrumbs
- ✓ 2 tablespoons vegetable oil

DIRECTIONS:

- ➢ In a pan of boiling water, add potatoes and cook for about 15 minutes.
- ➢ Drain the potatoes well and transfer into a large bowl.
- ➢ With a potato masher, mash the potatoes and set aside to cool completely.
- ➢ In the same bowl of mashed potatoes
- ➢ Add in the flour, Parmesan cheese, egg yolk
- ➢ Then chives, nutmeg, salt, and black pepper and mix until well combined.
- ➢ Make small equal-sized balls from the mixture.
- ➢ Now, roll each ball into a cylinder shape.
- ➢ In a shallow dish, crack the eggs and beat well.
- ➢ In another dish, mix together the breadcrumbs and oil.
- ➢ Dip the croquettes in egg mixture
- ➢ At this point coat with the breadcrumbs mixture.
- ➢ Arrange the "Crisper Basket" in the pot of Griller.
- ➢ Close the Griller with lid and select "Air Crisp".
- ➢ Set the temperature to 390 degrees F to preheat.
- ➢ Press "Start/Stop" to begin preheating.
- ➢ When the display shows "Add Food" open the lid
- ➢ Place the croquettes into the "Crisper
- ➢ Close the Griller with lid and set the time for 8 minutes.
- ➢ Press "Start/Stop" to begin cooking.
- ➢ When the cooking time is completed, press "Start/Stop" to stop cooking and open the lid.
- ➢ Serve warm.

79 GRILLED EGGPLANT AND PEPPER GOAT CHEESE SANDWICHES

Servings: 4   **Cook Time: 35 Min**   **Prep Time 10 Min**

INGREDIENTS:

- ✓ One red bell pepper
- ✓ One eggplant, sliced lengthwise into quarter-inch slices
- ✓ Three tbsp. low-fat bottled Italian
- ✓ You may also use balsamic vinaigrette
- ✓ Eight slices of whole-grain bread
- ✓ You may go for a French baguette cut lengthwise
- ✓ Two ounces soft goat cheese
- ✓ Quarter cup tapenade

DIRECTIONS:

- ➢ Preheat the grill medium-high.
- ➢ Cut off the bell pepper's top; discard the rind and seeds
- ➢ Get the pepper sliced into pieces
- ➢ Eggplant slices and bell pepper pieces are coated with low-fat bottled balsamic vinaigrette.
- ➢ On a grill covered with canola cooking spray
- ➢ Put the bell pepper pieces and eggplant slices
- ➢ Grill till tender plus slightly browned (8-10 minutes), about 6 inches from the fire, turning after 4-5 minutes.
- ➢ Spread four bottom bread slices with goat cheese
- ➢ Then with tapenade
- ➢ Cover with the slices of eggplant and a strip of red pepper the tapenade
- ➢ Then top with the remaining slices of bread.
- ➢ Cut each sandwich (if using whole-grain bread) into 2 or 4 triangles and eat.

80 GRILLED FAVA BEANS WITH MINT, LEMON ZEST AND SUMAC

Servings: 4　　　　　**Cook Time: 25 Min**　　　　　**Prep Time 5 Min**

INGREDIENTS:

- ✓ Twenty to thirty fresh Fava beans
- ✓ Olive oil for coating
- ✓ One pinch salt
- ✓ Three tbsp. olive oil
- ✓ One finely minced garlic clove
- ✓ One tbsp. finely chopped shallot
- ✓ One medium lemon zest
- ✓ Half teaspoon salt
- ✓ One tsp. sumac
- ✓ Quarter cup chopped fresh mint
- ✓ Quarter cup Italian Parsley
- ✓ Half teaspoon Aleppo chili
- ✓ One lemon juice

DIRECTIONS:

- ➢ Toss a little drizzle of olive oil with fava beans, just enough even to coat
- ➢ Sprinkle with salt generously.
- ➢ Grill each side until the grill marks become prominent (4-5 minutes, each side)
- ➢ Try out a tester to ensure that the inner bean is tender.
- ➢ Spread on a plate, spoon dressing over the top
- ➢ Sprinkle with parsley, Aleppo chili flakes and fresh mint
- ➢ You may taste one for salt.
- ➢ You may put lemon juice if you want more lemon taste.
- ➢ Eat with your fingers You can scrape out the beans with your teeth

81 KALE CHIPS

Servings: 4　　　　　**Cook Time: 20 Min**　　　　　**Prep Time 30 Min**

INGREDIENTS:

- ✓ 4 cups kale leaves
- ✓ Olive oil
- ✓ Salt to taste

DIRECTIONS:

- ➢ Drizzle kale with oil and sprinkle it with salt.
- ➢ Set the Pit basswood pellet grill to 250 degrees F.
- ➢ Preheat it for 15 minutes while the lid is closed.
- ➢ Add the kale leaves to a baking pan.
- ➢ Place the pan on the grill.
- ➢ Cook the kale for 20 minutes or until crispy.

82 POTATO FRIES WITH CHIPOTLE PEPPERS

Servings: 4　　　　　**Cook Time: 30 Min**　　　　　**Prep Time 30 Min**

INGREDIENTS:

- ✓ Four potatoes sliced into strips
- ✓ Three tablespoons olive oil
- ✓ Salt and pepper to taste
- ✓ 1 cup mayonnaise
- ✓ Two chipotle peppers in adobo sauce
- ✓ Two tablespoons lime juice

DIRECTIONS:

- ➢ Set the Pit basswood pellet grill to high.
- ➢ Preheat it for 15 minutes while the lid is closed.
- ➢ Coat the potato strips with oil.
- ➢ Sprinkle with salt and pepper.
- ➢ Put a baking pan on the grate.
- ➢ Transfer potato strips to the pan.
- ➢ Cook potatoes until crispy.
- ➢ Mix the remaining ingredients.
- ➢ Pulse in a food processor until pureed.
- ➢ Serve potato fries with chipotle dip.

83 GRILLED STRAWBERRY SHORTCAKE

Servings: 6   **Cook Time: 5 Min**   **Prep Time 15 Min**

INGREDIENTS:

- ✓ Two tablespoons powdered sugar
- ✓ Twelve ounces Angel Food Cake
- ✓ One-pound package of strawberries hulled (about 24)
- ✓ One and half cups whipping cream.
- ✓ Zest of 1 lemon
- ✓ Six skewers
- ✓ Mint leaves or Fresh basil for garnish (optional)
- ✓ Two tablespoons of honey

DIRECTIONS:

- ➢ In a medium bowl or the bowl of a stand mixer, pour the whipping cream.
- ➢ Whip the cream for 2-3 minutes on medium speed with a stand mixer or an eggbeater
- ➢ Add powdered sugar and lemon zest.
- ➢ Whip for another 4-6 minutes, or until soft peaks form
- ➢ Keep it in the fridge until serving.
- ➢ Preheat the grill to medium heat for direct cooking
- ➢ Then Angel food cake cut into six wedges.
- ➢ On each skewer, thread four strawberries.
- ➢ Drizzle one teaspoon honey over each strawberry skewer
- ➢ Spread it out with fingers or brush and coat the berries.
- ➢ Arrange the angel food cake and berry skewers on the grill
- ➢ Grill for 1-2 minutes on one side until grill marks appear
- ➢ Flip and grill for another 1-2 minutes, or until grill marks appear on the other side
- ➢ Remove from grill.
- ➢ Top each slice of angel food cake with about 1/2 cup whipped cream and a skewer of grilled strawberries.
- ➢ If you want, garnish with mint or basil leaves.

84 GRILLED S'MORE BANANA PACKETS

Serving: 1   **Cook Time: 15 Min**   **Prep Time 20 Min**

INGREDIENTS:

- ✓ Handful of marshmallows
- ✓ 1 banana
- ✓ 1 graham cracker
- ✓ Other additions, if desired: nuts, jam, peanut butter, Nutella, etc.
- ✓ Handful of chocolate chips

DIRECTIONS:

- ➢ Heat the grill about 350 degrees.
- ➢ Cut a small strip from the top of the banana peel with a knife, keeping one end intact
- ➢ Pull back the strip and cut a deep canyon down in the middle of the banana with a knife or spoon
- ➢ Eat the slice of banana you carve out.
- ➢ Add marshmallows, chocolate chips, and other toppings in the canyon as desired
- ➢ Fill it to the top
- ➢ Before you start, you can also smear some Biscoff spread or peanut butter.
- ➢ Set the peel back into place
- ➢ Then wrap a sheet of foil around the banana.
- ➢ Place the foil packets on the grill
- ➢ Cover, and cook for 10-12 minutes
- ➢ (Or until the chocolate and marshmallows are melted)
- ➢ Gently remove the foil from the grill
- ➢ Pull the peel back and enjoy!

85 GRILLED CHOCOLATE SANDWICHES

Servings: 6   Cook Time: 8 Min   Prep Time 5 Min

INGREDIENTS:

- ✓ 3 tbsps. Bing cherry preserves
- ✓ Twelve half-inch thick slices of challah, pound cake
- ✓ 1/3 cup unsalted melted butter.
- ✓ For garnish, use confectioners' sugar
- ✓ Two bittersweet chocolate bars, about 4-ounces, each cut into thirds (or you can also use milk chocolate)

DIRECTIONS:

- ➤ Preheat the grill, nonstick grill pan, or griddle to medium-low temperature.
- ➤ Set the bread or cake slices on the work surface
- ➤ Brush half atablespoon of cherry preserves on all six slices.
- ➤ Add one piece of chocolate on top of each brushed slice.
- ➤ Add the remaining bread or cake slices on top.
- ➤ Brush both sides of sandwiches with melted butter
- ➤ Then grill for 2 to 4 minutes per side
- ➤ (Or until the chocolate has melted and the bread turns to golden brown and crispy)
- ➤ Slice the sandwiches in quarters or half and serve warm
- ➤ Sprinkle some confectioners' sugar.

86 GRILLED SUMMER FRUIT SKEWERS

Servings: 8   Cook Time: 10 Min   Prep Time 15 Min

INGREDIENTS:

- ✓ 1 pt. Strawberries, sliced.
- ✓ 6 peaches, sliced.
- ✓ 8 skewers soaked in water for 20 minutes
- ✓ Extra-virgin olive oil for drizzling.
- ✓ 1 pineapple sliced into large cubes
- ✓ Honey, for drizzling.
- ✓ Kosher salt.

DIRECTIONS:

- ➤ Preheat the grill to medium-high heat.
- ➤ Skewer strawberries, pineapple, and peaches.
- ➤ Season with salt and drizzle with olive oil.
- ➤ Grill for 10 to 12 minutes, turning frequently until the fruit is slightly charred and tender.
- ➤ Drizzle honey on top.

87 EASY RUM-SOAKED GRILLED PINEAPPLE

Servings: 7   Cook Time: 10 Min   Prep Time 10 Min

INGREDIENTS:

- ✓ Half cup packed brown sugar
- ✓ Half cup dark rum
- ✓ 1 pineapple, cored and sliced into about 6-8 rings (choose desired thickness)
- ✓ 1 teaspoon ground cinnamon (plus extra for dusting)
- ✓ Favorite vanilla ice cream
- ✓ Cooking spray

DIRECTIONS:

- ➤ Combine the brown sugar, cinnamon, rum in a small bowl
- ➤ Then arrange the pineapple rings in a glass baking dish
- ➤ Pour the rum mixture over them
- ➤ Stir to coat, then set aside to soak for at least 15 minutes, tossing midway through.
- ➤ When you're about to cook the pineapple, drain the excess rum sauce from the pan
- ➤ Transfer it into a small saucepan
- ➤ Bring the sauce to a boil over medium-high heat
- ➤ Then decrease to medium- low heat
- ➤ Cook for 6-8 minutes, or until the sauce has been reduced by half and set aside.
- ➤ Heat a grill pan or sauté pan over medium-high heat while the sauce cooks
- ➤ Spray the pan lightly with cooking spray
- ➤ Cook for 1- 2 minutes per side until golden brown and grill marks appear
- ➤ Add pineapple slices in an even layer (you might need to do this in multiple pieces)
- ➤ Shift to a serving plate and set it aside
- ➤ Repeat with the rest of the pineapple.
- ➤ Drizzle rum sauce over each pineapple ring
- ➤ Top with a scoop of ice cream
- ➤ (You can also gently dust the pineapple with extra cinnamon if desired.)
- ➤ Serve right away.

88 BLACKOUT PEACH BREAD PUDDING

Servings: 6   **Cook Time: 15 Min**   **Prep Time 30 Min**

INGREDIENTS:

- ✓ 1 cup whole milk
- ✓ 4 large egg yolks
- ✓ 1/3 cup sugar
- ✓ Half tsp. ground cinnamon
- ✓ Two medium peaches halved and pitted
- ✓ Four halved potato dinner rolls.
- ✓ 1/4 cup mascarpone cheese
- ✓ 1 tbsp. melted butter.
- ✓ 2 tbsps. brown sugar
- ✓ Sweetened whipped cream (optional)
- ✓ Half cup caramel sundae syrup

DIRECTIONS:

- ➤ In a small bowl, whisk one cup whole milk, four large egg yolks, 1/4 cup mascarpone cheese, and 1/3 cup sugar
- ➤ (Until properly blended)
- ➤ Refrigerate until ready to use.
- ➤ Apply butter on peaches with a brush and grill while cover on
- ➤ Use a greased rack over medium heat for 5-6 minutes
- ➤ Rotate once, or broil 4 inches from heat until lightly browned. Uncover and grill for 3-4 minutes, rotating once, until lightly browned
- ➤ Let it cool for a little bit. Cut 3/4-inch cubes of peaches and rolls
- ➤ Add peaches and brown sugar to a big bowl, whisk in bread cubes
- ➤ Spoon into 12 disposable aluminum muffin cups that have been greased
- ➤ Fill muffin cups half with the egg mixture.
- ➤ Grill for 12-15 minutes, covered, over indirect high heat
- ➤ (Or until the thermometer measures at least 160°)
- ➤ Allow 5 minutes in the pan to cool before removing
- ➤ Present with caramel syrup and whipped cream, if you want.

Thank you for reading this book

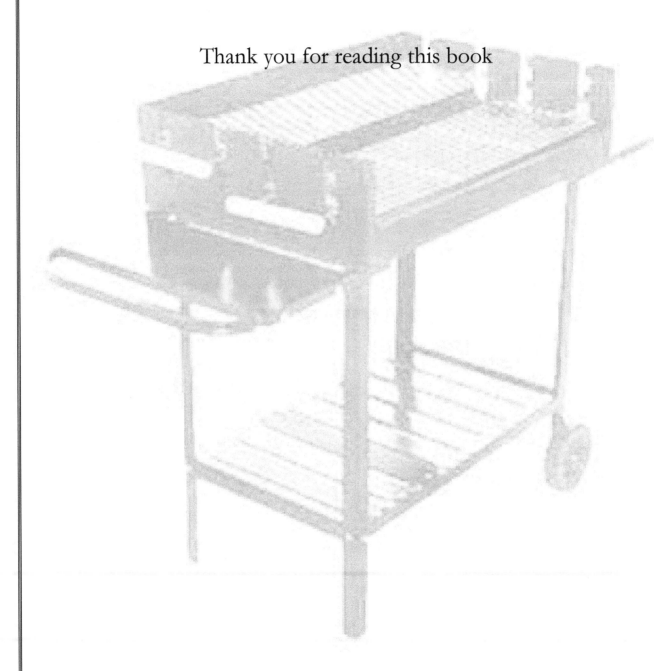

Lightning Source UK Ltd.
Milton Keynes UK
UKHW052324190421
382237UK00002BA/169